*I Love to Cook Book*

# I Love to Cook
# BOOK

## BY RUTH CONRAD BATEMAN

*The Ward Ritchie Press*
*Los Angeles*

To George and Connie

# PREFACE

The title of this book expresses my philosophy about cooking and things culinary in general. I love to cook—and wish everyone who is at all interested could get the same warm pleasure out of it I do. If you like to cook, you can be a good cook. Though you may not agree, I'm sure there's more to it than simply mastering the techniques. Honestly, did you ever know a really fine cook who hated his pots and pans?

This book is a result of an enthusiasm and curiosity that began so long ago I had to stand tip-toe on a box to reach the cabinet. I recall it well—and the floury biscuits I produced. Although it contains a number of such recipes, this is not a basic cookbook. It is a collection of unusual and special recipes, somewhat adventuresome and, in a few cases, completely unorthodox. I have made and loved them, every one. And struggled sincerely to put on paper directions you could follow with success. I hope you'll find them exciting and fun to make.

I am grateful to the following for permission to include in this book a number of recipes previously developed for them: California Foods Research Institute, J. Walter Thompson Company and Better Homes & Gardens.

My warm thanks to Helen Evans Brown for her expert counsel and immeasurable help on the manuscript, to Marka Ritchie and Jo Hartley for enthusiastic editorial assistance, to Elena Quinn and Marion Raymond for faithful hours of typing, and to all my friends, family and the restaurants who have been generous with recipes and ideas.

To my husband, George Bateman, who has sustained me through the trials of testing, and rendered a refreshing "man's viewpoint," my greatest thanks are due.

RUTH CONRAD BATEMAN

Whittier, California, 1962

# CONTENTS

# INTRODUCTION

*It was about ten years ago that I first met Ruth Conrad Bateman. I do not recall the occasion, but I remember her vividly. She is that kind of a person—warm, colorful, unassuming, and attractive. She was dressed in a costume of the Gay Nineties (it was that kind of a party) and was having a whirl. She obviously loved everyone, and everyone loved her. It was later that I learned she also loved to cook and was, therefore, a superb one. Ruth's professional training and long experience in recipe development for various food companies, advertising agencies, and magazines has, no doubt, contributed to her skill as a cook (practice does help make perfect), but I think her real talent arises from the fact that she has all the attributes of a cordon bleu—curiosity, patience, a willingness to work hard, a fine palate, and, most of all, a great passion for cooking.*

*Anyone who has had the delight of being a guest in the Batemans' charming house in Whittier will vouch for their abilities as hosts. George's affable attention to his guests in no way overshadows his infinite pride in his lovely wife's culinary triumphs. What's more, he enjoys eating Ruth's food as much as she likes to cook it. But then, so do we all.*

*In this book you may find familiar recipes, but each one has a little original touch, the touch that only Ruth Bateman's love of cooking could have produced. I am sure that it will become one of your favorite cookbooks, and that when you use it you, too, will love to cook.*

HELEN EVANS BROWN

*I Love to Cook Book*

# Appetizers

You can do a lot towards breaking the ice at your party and helping guests to feel at ease with the kind of hors d'oeuvre and potables you serve. Accessories are a big help too. Conversation will fly when everyone elbows around your miniature hibachi to barbecue shrimp, meat balls, or whatever savory you provide. A bountiful cheese board with some really big pieces of cheese—say a whole one—looks much more opulent and the cheese tastes so much better than dabby little dried-out bites. Provide an assortment of crisp crackers, good breads, and cheese knives for do-it-yourself appetizers.

### SHRIMP OCEANO

One of the simplest ways to cook shrimp—with fresh lime juice and salt. And one of the best! We enjoyed them first in the leafy bay-front patio of Hotel Oceano in our particular paradise, Puerto Vallarta, Mexico.

*There they use their own wonderful camarones, fresh limes, and moist, coarse sea salt.*

Split 1½ pounds fresh jumbo shrimp in half lengthwise through the shell and tail. Rinse out dark vein. Dry shrimp on paper towels, place in flat dish and sprinkle cut side generously with juice of 1 or 2 fresh limes. Sprinkle with about 2 teaspoons coarse kosher salt. Let stand in refrigerator a couple of hours, if possible.

At serving time, heat 2 to 3 tablespoons mild salad oil in large heavy skillet. Add about half the shrimp at a time, sauté until shells are pink, no more than 2 or 3 minutes on each side. Heap onto a warm platter with lots of quartered fresh limes. Serve shrimp as hot appetizer to 6, or as supper entrée for 3. Pass small plates with appetizer—and plenty of paper napkins. Or another thoughtful gesture—pass a tray of finger tip towels, dipped in hot water, wrung dry and rolled tightly.

### OLIVE EMPANADITAS

*Make and fill these miniature pastries ahead of time and keep in the refrigerator on cooky sheets. Bake as the party progresses so you can serve them hot.*

Make a rich pastry dough using 1½ cups flour (or use packaged pie crust mix). Mix ⅔ cup grated sharp Cheddar cheese and ⅔ cup chopped ripe olives with ¾ teaspoon good chili powder, a pinch of crumbled oregano. Roll dough thin and cut with 2½-inch biscuit cutter. Put a dab of filling on half of each round, fold over in half-moon shapes. Moisten edges and pinch together to seal. Place on cooky sheets. Bake in very hot oven (475°) 10 to 12 minutes. Serve hot. Makes about 3 dozen.

### SPICY RIPE OLIVES

Combine 1 can jumbo or mammoth size ripe olives and liquid with 1 tablespoon mixed pickling spices, 2 tablespoons vinegar (tarragon is nice) and 1 chopped clove garlic. Bring just to boil. Cover and remove from heat. Cool, then refrigerate overnight or several days in glass jar or refrigerator dish with lid. Before serving toss with a spoonful olive oil, finely minced parsley. Pass with cocktail picks.

4

CRACKED GREEN OLIVES

*We kept ourselves broke buying these until Joe Simonetti, owner of our favorite delicatessen, taught us how to make them.*

Crack imported green Italian olives by squashing soundly with the bottom of a heavy jar or bottle. Hit them several blows, if necessary, to crack the olive open and expose the meat. For 1 pint, chop coarsely a generous ½ cup each white onion and celery and tops. Mix with olives and about 1 tablespoon fine Italian olive oil, a pinch of oregano, a mere hint of crushed garlic—not over ¼ clove, and 1 to 2 teaspoons lively red wine vinegar. Marinate until flavors penetrate olives, a few hours or several days. Serve as relish or appetizer with picks.

HACIENDA BEAN DIP

*If green salsa Jalapeña is not available in your community, season the bean dip with any of the more familiar red chili sauces such as taco sauce or Mexican chili sauce, available in Mexican or specialty shops.*

> 2 cloves garlic, crushed
> ¾ teaspoon salt, or to taste
> 3 cups Mexican fried beans (frijoles fritos*)—home cooked or canned
> 2 tablespoons Mexican hot sauce or green salsa Jalapeña
> 2 tablespoons fresh bacon drippings or soft butter
> ¾ cup grated sharp Cheddar cheese
> ¼ cup sour cream

Crush garlic and salt together by pressing against sides of bowl with wooden spoon. Add beans and rest of ingredients except sour cream. Vary amount of hot sauce according to your taste. Just before serving put in top of double boiler and heat enough to melt cheese. Stir in sour cream. Serve warm, *not hot*, in a Mexican pottery bowl over a candle warmer if you have it. Accompany with giant-size corn chips or crisp-fried, quartered tortillas. If you can't find any of the Mexican hot sauces, season bean dip with 2 dried red peppers crushed in a spoonful of hot water with 2 teaspoons chili powder.

*To make homemade Mexican fried beans (frijoles fritos):* Soak 1 cup California pink, Mexican red, or pinto beans several hours or overnight. Simmer gently in about 3½ cups water until very tender, about 2 hours. Add 1 teaspoon salt last half hour. Mash part of the beans against sides of the pan with a big wooden spoon. Stir into ¼ cup bacon drippings in heavy pan or skillet. Add more beans and liquid and stir over very low heat till all the beans and liquid are used. Continue to cook and stir until the mixture is about consistency of thick mush.

### INDIVIDUAL QUICHE

*Cocktail miniatures of famous Quiche Lorraine with a western accent.*

>      Rich pastry dough (basic 1½ cup recipe)
>     6 slices crisp bacon
>     6 ounces aged Swiss cheese, grated
>     2 teaspoons flour
>     ½ cup sliced ripe olives or mushrooms
>     ½ cup minced onion
>     2 tablespoons butter
>     2 eggs
>     1 cup cream or milk
>     ¾ teaspoon salt
>      Dash each nutmeg and cayenne

Roll pastry thin and cut into 3-inch rounds with cooky cutter or scalloped pastry wheel. (You should get 18 to 24.) Fit into bottom of small (2-inch) muffin pans. Crumble bacon and mix with cheese, flour, and olives. Divide among pans. Saute onion in butter. Beat eggs until foamy; add milk, seasonings, onion. Pour over cheese in pans. Bake in hot oven (425°) about 7 minutes. Reduce heat to 300°. Bake about 10 minutes longer, or until set. Cool at least 10 minutes before removing from pans. Serve warm. Delicious reheated.

### SEVICHE, PUERTO VALLARTA

*This appetizer of "lime-cooked" raw fish is made a little differently in Puerto Vallarta than in Acapulco. In this beautifully unspoiled tropical village on Mexico's west coast, they use their delicate white Sierra fish— a member of the Spanish king mackerel family. It is scraped into shreds and seems to absorb the lime juice more quickly—has a sharper flavor.*

Start with about 2 pounds fresh fish (any firm-fleshed white fish such as sea bass will do). Remove skin from fish and lay it on board. Hold a sharp heavy French knife at a 45° angle, and scrape it over the fish, slicing off paper-thin pieces that fall apart as you cut. The fish falls in tiny particles of "grated" fish. Measure 4 cups and place in glass dish. Cover with about 2 cups fresh lime juice. Add it gradually, "as much as the fish will take," the natives say. When all the fish has turned white "or been cooked by the acid of the juice," that's enough. This usually takes from several minutes to ½ hour. Now add 2 finely chopped onions, 2 peeled, seeded finely chopped tomatoes. Mix well and season to taste with salt and some type of Mexican sauce—such as taco sauce or salsa Jalapeña. Chill several hours. Drain off excess liquid. Serve with salty crackers, corn chips, or fried quartered tortillas.

### PICKLED SWORDFISH

*A low-calorie appetizer, greatly appreciated by those who try to avoid the rich dips and spreads so often served with drinks.*

> 2 cups good cider vinegar
> 2 cups water
> 1¼ teaspoons salt
> 1 thinly sliced lemon
> 2 sliced onions
> 2 bay leaves
> 1 dozen whole black peppercorns
> 1½ dozen whole allspice
> ¼ teaspoon dill seeds
> 1 pound swordfish steaks

Combine all the ingredients except 1 of the sliced onions and the swordfish. Simmer 15 minutes. Add swordfish steaks, 1 at a time, and simmer 5 to 7 minutes. Remove from spiced vinegar. Cut into 1-inch cubes for appetizers. Place in glass or earthenware dish. Add remaining sliced onion and the boiling vinegar. Cover. Cool. Refrigerate at least overnight. Serve on cocktail picks as appetizer. Pass a bowl of seasoned mayonnaise or sour cream for dunking, if you like, but it's wonderful just as is. Marinate swordfish without cubing for salad or cold entrée.

7

RUMAKI PÂTÉ

*A delicious cocktail spread with the seasonings and ingredients of the famous broiled rumaki.*

>½ pound fresh or frozen chicken livers
>2 tablespoons butter
>6 slices lean smoky bacon
>1 can water chestnuts or
>>1 cup peeled and chopped, fresh water chestnuts
>1 teaspoon grated onion
>1 teaspoon soy sauce
>¼ cup cream
>¼ cup sour cream
>Freshly ground black pepper

Sauté fresh or just-thawed chicken livers in butter lightly, until tinged with brown but still moist and a little pinkish inside. Chop finely. In same skillet fry bacon crisp, drain and crumble into livers. Add finely chopped water chestnuts and rest of ingredients. Taste and add salt if needed . . . depends on saltiness of the bacon. Chill but remove from refrigerator and serve at room temperature with crackers or toast strips. Add more cream if it gets too dry and solid.

FINNAN HADDIE BALLS

*Make and fry these fish puffs the day before the party, then reheat on cooky sheets in a moderately hot oven.*

>1½ cups flaked poached finnan haddie*
>2 cups mashed potatoes
>2 tablespoons butter
>1 teaspoon Worcestershire sauce
>6 dashes Tabasco sauce
>3 eggs, separated
>1 whole egg, beaten
>Fine dry bread crumbs
>Oil for deep fat frying

*\*To poach fish:* Put finnan haddie into a shallow pan with a little water in the bottom. Punch hole in a piece of waxed paper cut to fit top of pan; place over fish. Cover with lid. Steam fish until tender, 5 to 8 minutes. Flake and measure 1½ cups. Mix with potatoes, melted butter,

8

seasonings, 2 to 4 tablespoons liquor from fish, and the beaten egg yolks. Fold in stiffly whipped egg whites. Shape into 5 or 6 dozen tiny balls. Dip in egg beaten with a little water, then in fine dry bread crumbs. Heat deep fat to 375°. Fry balls golden brown. Serve hot from chafing dish with cocktail picks.

ANCHOVY PIROSHKI

*Nibble-size turnovers inspired by Russian meat-filled piroshki. May be made ahead and chilled before baking. In fact, chilling improves the flaky texture of the cream cheese pastry.*

> 1 3-ounce package cream cheese
> 1 package pie crust mix
> 2 hard-cooked eggs
> 1 tin flat anchovy fillets
> 2 teaspoons instant minced onion
> 1 tablespoon cream
> ½ cup chopped ripe olives
> 2 tablespoons mayonnaise
> 1 teaspoon hot prepared mustard

Work cream cheese into pie crust mix with fork. Mix by label directions using a little less water. Wrap in waxed paper; chill 1 hour. Chop eggs. Drain anchovies; chop finely. Mix both with rest of ingredients (no salt please). Cut chilled dough in half. Roll thin and cut with 2½-inch round cutter. Put teaspoonful filling on each round, a little off center. Fold over and press edges together with tines of fork. Bake in moderately hot oven (375°) 15 minutes. Makes about 5 to 6 dozen piroshki. Serve warm.

CHICKEN CHESTNUT BALLS

*Almond coated tidbits with a delicate curry flavor.*

Grind with the finest blade of the food chopper 1 cup cooked chicken or turkey (white meat preferred). Chop enough water chestnuts to make ½ cup. Mix with chicken. Add 1 teaspoon curry powder and mayonnaise to moisten. Salt lightly and form into tiny balls. Roll in finely chopped, toasted almonds. Chill thoroughly. Serve on cocktail picks.

# Bring Out Your Soup Tureen

---

Soup tureens are high style. Get yours out and use it—for your family, for parties. You can make quite a ceremony of soup, salad, and home-made bread and become famous for entertaining in this way.

### LIMA CARAWAY SOUP

This is impressive when served from a big white tureen with hefty floats of sliced knackwurst and flecks of minced watercress.

    1 cup dry lima beans
    ¼ cup pearl barley
    8 cups beef stock

   1 chopped onion
   ¼ teaspoon monosodium glutamate
   ½ teaspoon caraway seeds
      Dash garlic salt
      Salt and pepper
   2 sliced knackwurst
      Minced parsley or watercress

Soak lima beans and barley overnight. Simmer in boiling stock with onion till tender, about 1½ hours. Mash part of the beans; leave remainder whole. Stir in seasonings adding salt and pepper to taste at last. Sprinkle in the thinly sliced knackwurst. Simmer for 5 minutes. Serve with a topping of minced parsley or water cress. Makes about 2½ quarts soup.

## CREAM OF LENTIL SOUP

*You will have some of these good lentils left over. Serve them as they do at San Francisco's famous German restaurant, Shroeders—cooked down until quite dry, then heaped onto a plate with garlic sausage.*

   1 pound dried lentils
   1½ quarts water
   ½ cup chopped celery
   1 onion
   1 dried red pepper
   1 sprig fresh thyme (or ¼ teaspoon dried)
   2 tablespoons chopped parsley
1 to 2 teaspoons salt
   3 cups milk
   2 thinly sliced green onions
   1 cup cream
      Minced parsley

*To cook lentils:* Cover lentils with water. Add celery, onion, red pepper, thyme, and parsley. Cook gently about 2 hours. Add salt after first hour, adjusting amount.

*To make soup:* Force enough lentils through coarse sieve to make 3 cups purée. Heat milk and green onions just until bubbles show around

11

edges. Stir into lentils. Add cream, and cook gently until very hot and smooth. Add salt, if needed, and freshly ground black pepper. Ladle into bowls or soup tureen. Top with minced parsley. Makes 6 servings.

MEAT BORSCH

*Half stew—half soup, with the traditional sweet-sour seasonings of sugar and lemon juice. It was given us by an Ukranian friend.*

> 3 pounds beef (chuck pot roast or brisket) or 4 pounds meaty
>     short ribs
> 1 shank soup bone
> 3 quarts water
> 2 leeks, chopped
> 1 clove garlic, chopped
> 2 tablespoons salt
> 1 bay leaf
> 2 onions, sliced
> 2 stalks celery, sliced
> 4 small carrots, sliced
> ½ small head cabbage, cubed
> 1 no. 2½ can tomatoes
> 4 raw beets, pared and diced
> 2 tablespoons sugar
> 3 tablespoons lemon juice
>     Coarse black pepper
> 1 raw beet, peeled and shredded
> 1½ cups sour cream

*Day before:* Cut meat into 6 or 8 pieces. Put into large deep kettle, with soup bone, water, leeks, garlic, salt, and bay leaf. Cover and simmer until tender, 2 hours or longer. Cool uncovered.

*Next morning:* Skim off excess fat. Cut meat into bite-sized chunks (remove bones, if you like, but we leave them in for flavor till the last). Add onions, celery, carrots, cabbage, tomatoes, and diced beets. Simmer covered about 1½ hours. Scoop out the bones. Season soup with sugar, lemon juice, and lots of coarse black pepper. If you've never made this before, taste as you add the sweet and sour till it suits you. Add the

12

shredded beet. Simmer about 30 minutes to blend flavors. Pour carefully into warm soup tureen or large casserole. Ladle hot into big warm soup bowls. Top each with a spoonful of sour cream. Makes 8 to 10 man-size servings.

### MARION'S BELGIAN PEA SOUP

*Marion Raymond, who helped type this book, gave us this recipe of her brother's. He got it from a friendly Belgian woman who served him welcome cups of it on wintry nights in World War II when he was doing guard duty.*

> ½ pound dried green split peas
> 3 quarts water
> 1 soup bone or cracked ham bone
> 2 laurel (bay) leaves
> 1 pound potatoes
> 2 or 3 leeks or 1 onion
> 3 or 4 stalks celery and tops
>   Salt and pepper

Soak peas overnight. Drain. Add water, soup bone and bay leaves. Bring to boil. Skim off foam. Add potatoes, leeks or onion, and celery, cut in large pieces to fit into pot. Simmer gently for about 2 hours. Press through sieve. Season with salt and pepper to taste. Cook for 15 minutes, stirring occasionally. Makes 8 to 10 servings.

### OUR CHUNKY SPLIT PEA SOUP

*Made like the soup above except we don't sieve it. Must it always be? We wondered once, and discovered it's interesting the other way.*

Simmer soaked split peas with a ham bone, garlic, 1 onion, a bay leaf, and some whole pepper as above. Remove bone. Season soup with salt then add chopped carrots, onion, and celery. Simmer about 1 hour longer, or until vegetables are tender. Some of the peas stay whole, some disintegrate. Delicious.

*A simple pot of soup—savory, fragrant and delicious. It's as American as the Fourth of July but can be given an entirely different character by a change of vegetables, herb seasoning, the kind of meat you use.*

> 1 meaty beef shank or 2 neck bones
> 1 soup bone (shin bone is good)
> 2 quarts water
> 2 onions, sliced
> 1 tablespoon salt
> 4 whole cloves
> 4 small carrots, sliced
> 2 stalks celery, sliced

One or all of following may be added. Each gives a different flavor and character to the basic beef vegetable soup.

> 1 cup canned or fresh tomatoes
> 1 cup shredded cabbage
> 2 small potatoes, diced, or a handful dry macaroni
> ½ cup peas or cut green beans
> Herbs ad lib—parsley, bay leaf, thyme
> Freshly ground black pepper

Combine beef shank, soup bone, water, onions, salt, and cloves in deep soup kettle. Simmer slowly until meat is tender, 2 hours or longer. Add prepared vegetables and herbs. Leave out beans or peas till half hour before soup is served. Sprinkle in more salt for the vegetables and plenty of freshly ground black pepper. Taste for amounts. Simmer until vegetables are tender and flavor is rich and soupy—1½ to 2 hours. If needed, add water occasionally. Remove bones and break meat into chunky bites with fork. Serve in warm bowls with crusty bread and a big salad of snowy cottage cheese with your favorite fruit and greenery. Makes 6 to 8 servings.

*French butter trick:* If the meat is not flavorful enough to make a rich, deep-flavored stock, drop 1 to 2 tablespoons butter into soup at the last and let it simmer a few minutes to melt and enrich the soup flavor.

CRAB BISQUE

*Creamy pink perfection—and in a matter of minutes. Finely diced avo-cado adds a pleasant surprise.*

    1 cup crab meat in big pieces (fresh, frozen, or canned)
    2 cans frozen cream of shrimp soup
    1 soup-can milk
    1 soup-can cream
      Salt and pepper
      Generous dash nutmeg
    2 tablespoons sherry wine
    1 soft-ripe avocado
    2 teaspoons lemon juice

Defrost frozen crab meat barely enough to separate. Break into chunks. In top of double boiler heat soup, milk, and cream very slowly. Spoon milk over soup as it heats and melts. It may look curdled, but will stir out as you mix and heat. Stir in crab meat, and season with salt, freshly ground pepper, sherry, and nutmeg. When hot and just before serving, add finely diced avocado and lemon juice. Heat 1 minute longer but do not boil. Serve to 4.

*To serve chilled instead:* Press avocado through a sieve and stir into bisque after removing from heat. Blend well and chill.

CHICKEN IVORY

*A beautiful pale chicken soup richly laced with cream and egg yolks, with a hint of spice. The perfect soup to serve for a very important luncheon.*

    2 tablespoons cornstarch
    ¼ teaspoon marjoram
    ¼ teaspoon curry powder
      Generous dash nutmeg
    4 cups rich, strong chicken stock
    4 egg yolks
    1 cup cream
      Salt
      Chives

Mix cornstarch, marjoram, curry powder, and nutmeg with a little cold water to a smooth paste. Stir into chicken stock. Cook over low heat, stirring with a wire whisk until smooth and thickened and cornstarch is cooked completely. Beat egg yolks till thick and pale lemon colored. Add cream to soup. Heat to boiling, but do not boil. Spoon some of hot soup into yolks. Mix and pour back into soup, stirring constantly with wire whisk, over very low heat 3 to 4 minutes longer. Season lightly with salt. Pour into warm bowls over a few snipped chives. Makes 4 to 5 servings.

## MEAT BALL SOUP

*Little savory meat balls are simmered in a rich beef stock flavored with a bit of red wine.*

    ½ pound ground beef
    ¼ pound bulk pork sausage
    ¾ cup fine dry bread crumbs
    1 beaten egg
    ¾ cup milk
    1 tablespoon grated onion
    ½ teaspoon salt
    ¼ teaspoon pepper
    ¼ teaspoon allspice
    ½ cup sliced onions
    2 tablespoons butter
  2½ quarts rich beef stock
    1 cup dry red wine

Combine first 9 ingredients. Shape into walnut-size balls. Let stand in refrigerator for an hour. Separate onions into rings; sauté in butter until golden. Bring stock and wine to boil in deepish rather wide pan, so the meat balls won't be crowded. Gently drop in meat balls and onions. Cover and simmer 15 to 20 minutes. Do not overcook. Spoon meat balls into soup bowls, pour hot soup over them. Makes about 6 servings.

## EMERALD POTATO SOUP

*A thick and creamy soup that looks and tastes elegant, but can be made in a hurry with frozen potato soup and spinach.*

16

In a saucepan combine 1 can frozen cream-of-potato soup, 1 cup chicken broth or stock, 2 chopped green onions and tops, and ½ package frozen chopped spinach (return rest to package to use later). Cover and heat slowly until thawed; stir frequently. Simmer a few minutes to cook spinach. Add ½ teaspoon dried marjoram leaves and buzz in blender until smooth. You can mix this fairly smooth on electric mixer or with a rotary beater but blender is easier and faster. Add ½ cup milk, ½ cup cream, a little salt and freshly ground pepper. Return to saucepan. Heat gently until bubbly, but don't let it boil. Should serve 3 but two can make a meal of it with crusty bread and a crisp salad.

*For an unusual emerald "Vichyssoise":* Use all cream in place of part milk, season gently with nutmeg instead of marjoram, and chill.


## AVOCADO CLAM VELVET

*Here's a glacier-cool blend of clams, cream, and avocado.*

> 2 large soft-ripe avocados (2 cups diced)
> 1 cup cream
> ½ cup minced clams and liquor
> ½ cup chilled chicken stock (fresh, canned, or from chicken
>     bouillon cubes)
> Lemon juice
> Salt and cayenne pepper
> Snipped chives

Cut avocados into halves, remove seed and skin. Dice fruit to make 2 cups. Beat smooth with rotary beater; slowly beat in cream. Blend in clams and chicken stock. Beat until smooth as velvet (or buzz in blender). Season with a drop or two of lemon juice, salt to taste, and a flick of cayenne pepper. Serve in chilled bowls with snipped chives on top. Makes 4 servings.


## CHILLED BROCCOLI SOUP

*An unusual vegetable soup accented with rosemary. Delicious served cold—or hot!*

> 1 onion, chopped
> 1 carrot, chopped

½ cup celery, chopped
2 cups water
1 package frozen chopped broccoli
3 cups chicken stock
Salt and pepper
2 tablespoons cornstarch
1 cup cream
Snipped fresh rosemary or a few dried rosemary leaves, crushed

Simmer onion, carrot, and celery in the water 15 minutes. Cook broccoli 5 minutes. Drain and add to vegetables. Stir in chicken stock. Season to taste with salt and pepper. Simmer until very tender and flavors are blended. Thicken with cornstarch moistened in a little cold water. Force through sieve or strainer. Chill well. Blend in table cream. Serve in chilled bowls with a sprinkle of rosemary on top. Makes 4 servings. *Some like it hot:* Blend cream into thickened puréed vegetables. Season with rosemary and heat gently, but do not boil.

# The Well-Dressed Salad

Far from being a big production, a good salad can be very simple . . . a plate of juicy red tomatoes . . . a few silvery sticks of celery . . . a golden orange symmetrically sliced . . . or a bowl of cool fresh greens. Freshness is the key—and a dressing to enhance, not overpower.

Since mixed greens mean "salad" to most of us, I've gone into some detail about what goes into it, tricks in tossing, seasoning, and such. It's much ado about a simple little salad, but this is the basis of all your salad making. Once you've mastered the technique of tossing a salad and mixing the dressing as you toss it, you can make any salad a masterpiece!

### SALAD GREENS

There's a wonderful world of lettuce, you know, besides plain "Head!" Combine several kinds if you possibly can, because each contributes its own unique taste and texture.

19

For instance, contrast the crisp, elongated leaves of romaine with tender butter lettuce—or Boston or Bibb. Try feathery leaf or garden lettuce together with the mild chunky iceberg. Introduce something quite distinctive . . . like the almost bitter tang of curly endive or chicory . . . or the deep color of young spinach or watercress. And when you can find it, and feel extravagant, splurge with the elegant, pale, Belgian endive.

*Oils and vinegars:* Fine imported olive oil adds a definite finesse and delicacy. Since the best is expensive, I usually combine it with mild salad oil, such as corn oil. Red wine vinegar, fresh and living, mixed with a little tarragon vinegar is my choice for greens. Some of the herb vinegars are also interesting.

*Freshly ground pepper:* Grinding pepper fresh onto your salad releases the pungent flavor and aroma exactly when and where you want it. There's no comparison between this and ready-ground pepper in the real excitement and zest it will add.

*Salt:* Salt mills are to be had now also. Once you try them, you'll become a freshly-ground-salt fan too. Most beginners do not use enough salt in their salad bowls. It's a very important key and can make the difference between a truly inspired salad and a flat, insipid bowl of leaves.

*Herbs and spices:* The subtle use of thoughtfully chosen herbs or spices might well become the hallmark of your salads, the thing that makes them yours. Use most sparingly—less than you think. Try sweet basil with tomatoes; tarragon to accent fish, chicken or eggs; mint, anise, or cardamon for fruit and melon mixtures. A dash of curry powder, dry mustard, or red pepper adds sharpness and zest to almost all vegetable combinations.

## How to Toss the Salad

1. *Have greens dry and cold.* The oil can not coat wet leaves. Your salad will be limp and tastless and the dressing will end up in the bottom of the bowl. After sorting and washing (be *ruthless* here!), blot greens with paper towels, then wrap in towel and chill crisp. (You may break into pieces now—but do not cut with a knife as leaf edges will turn brown.)

2. *Use a jumbo-size salad bowl.* Wood is best! It's porous and absorbs the essence of seasonings, then releases them again into your salad. It's impossible to toss greens properly without at least 4 or 5 inches "head-room," so splurge on a really big bowl. Wipe dry, or rinse in warm water after each use and *dry it thoroughly.* Never use soap!

3. *Add a bit of garlic.* If omitted, this indispensable flavor will be missed even by confirmed non-garlic fans. Crush a cut clove with the tip of a spoon against sides of bowl until it disappears. Or do as the French do. Rub small pieces of rather dry bread with cut garlic clove, then toss these little "chapons" with the salad.

4. *Toss with oil first* until all leaves are shiny and coated. This seals in flavor, seals out flavor-robbing air. Adding the vinegar first will wilt the greens.

5. *Now, sprinkle with vinegar,* and your salt and pepper, a little at a time. The dressing may be mixed ahead and poured on, but this way is preferred by connoisseurs.

6. *Toss plenty and taste as you go along.* Lift greens lightly from bottom of bowl with fork and spoon. Keep tasting before all the vinegar and seasonings are used. You'll soon learn exactly how much.

7. *Add wet ingredients last.* Tomatoes, cucumbers, fruits, any drippy foods will dilute the dressing and crush the greens if added too soon.

8. *Serve salad immediately*—while fresh, crisp and lively! Try it the western way, as a first course. This custom allows you to serve the salad the minute it's tossed. As you may gather, I feel rather strongly about green salads!


THE GLORIOUS SALAD BOWL—HERE IT IS!

 2 quarts mixed greens, broken up (about 2 heads each romaine
  and butter lettuce)
 6 branches chicory or curly endive
  Few sprays watercress
 1 clove garlic, crushed
 3 green onions or scallions, sliced

4 to 6 tablespoons salad oil
        (half olive oil—half corn oil)
1½ to 2 teaspoons salt
        4 teaspoons red wine vinegar
        1 teaspoon tarragon vinegar
            Freshly ground black pepper
            Radishes and cucumbers, thinly sliced

Toss as already directed. Makes 4 to 6 servings.


## SPINACH SALAD BOWL

*This salad is best served the second it's tossed—while greens and bacon are crisp. Perfect with macaroni and cheese and hot corn muffins.*

        2 cups chopped raw spinach
        2 cups cubed iceberg lettuce
        3 sliced green onions
        2 chopped hard-cooked eggs
        ½ cup sliced ripe olives
            Salt and pepper
        4 slices bacon, diced
        3 tablespoons cider and red wine vinegars mixed
        1 teaspoon sugar
        1 teaspoon Worcestershire sauce

Put crisp chilled spinach and lettuce in salad bowl. Top with green onions, eggs, and ripe olives. Sprinkle lightly with salt and pepper. Fry bacon crisp; drain on paper towel. Pour bacon drippings into cup. Measure out 3 tablespoons and put back into skillet. Heat, and add vinegar, sugar, and Worcestershire. Heat to boiling and pour hot over the salad; add diced bacon and toss until well mixed. Add salt and pepper if needed. Serve at once while bacon is crisp. Makes 3 to 4 servings.


## GREEN SALAD, FANTASIA

*The lively avocado dressing gives this salad its name. Ideal for summer parties.*

For about 1½ cups dressing, mash 1 soft-ripe avocado with fork so you'll still have some lumps of avocado. Add 2 finely diced small tomatoes,

2 teaspoons grated onion, 1½ to 2 tablespoons anchovy paste, ¼ cup vinegar, ½ cup salad oil. Blend well. Season with a few grindings black pepper and sprinkling of salt. Pour over torn salad greens . . . crisp iceberg lettuce, romaine, Boston, or Bibb lettuce and a few tender spinach leaves. Toss like crazy . . . (dressing may darken a little, but it's still delicious if kept several days in refrigerator).

GREENS AND FRUIT, CHIVE DRESSING

*This would be a perfect salad to serve with* MEAT BORSCH *and home-made* BUTTERMILK RYE BREAD. *(See index.)*

Shake together in covered jar: ⅓ cup salad oil, 1½ tablespoons red wine vinegar, 1 teaspoon salt, 1½ teaspoons lemon juice, ½ teaspoon each grated lemon and orange rind, ½ teaspoon sugar, 2 tablespoons snipped chives. Put your choice of chilled, torn salad greens in a big salad bowl. (1 romaine, 1 Boston or Bibb, 1 watercress would be nice.) Pour on the dressing and toss lightly. Add more salt if needed. Peel and slice 2 chilled oranges. Cut slices in half and lay in circle on top of greens. Wash and pull from stems a small bunch of chilled seedless green grapes. Sprinkle over salad bowl.

BUFFET ARTICHOKE PLATTER

*An effective way to serve artichokes for a buffet or other informal party. This makes a good first course.*

> 3 large artichokes
>    Salt, salad oil, wine vinegar
> 3 cups cooked crab meat (legs are best) or large shrimp
>    Small leaves butter lettuce
> 1½ cups mayonnaise
> 1½ teaspoons Worcestershire sauce
>    1 tablespoon lemon juice, or to taste
>    Lemon wedges

Cook artichokes in a big pot of boiling salted water to which you've added a tablespoon each of salad oil and vinegar. Cook about 45 minutes, until a center leaf pulls out easily. Drain upside down and chill.

Chill crab or shrimp. At serving time split artichokes lengthwise and scoop out the fuzzy "choke" with a teaspoon. Alternate artichoke halves with small lettuce leaves on big round chop plate. Heap artichokes with crab or shrimp. Pep up mayonnaise with Worcestershire sauce and lemon juice to taste. Place in bowl in center of plate. Let each guest help himself to an artichoke half and a lettuce leaf. Fill lettuce with mayonnaise for dunking crab and artichoke leaves. Provide plenty of extra lemon wedges and paper napkins. Makes 6 salads.

## ICED DILL BEANS

*Pickled green beans with the fragrance of dill. Serve as relish, salad, or a low-calorie hors d'oeuvre.*

> 4 cups cut fresh green beans (about 2 pounds)
> 2 cups boiling salted water
> 1 cup tarragon vinegar
> ¼ cup brown sugar
> 1 bay leaf
> 1 clove garlic, minced
> 1 teaspoon dill seeds
> 1 large white Bermuda onion

String fresh tender beans and snap into 2-inch pieces. Cook in boiling salted water until crisp-tender, about 10 minutes. With slotted spoon remove beans to glass jar or covered refrigerator dish. To 2 cups bean cooking liquid add rest of ingredients, except onion. Simmer 5 to 8 minutes. Slice onion paper thin onto beans. Cover with boiling hot liquid. Cover and refrigerate several days. Serve as relish, cold vegetable, or as salad in lettuce cups with sliced tomatoes and hard-cooked eggs. Makes 3 to 4 servings.

*Canned dill beans:* Drain beans and add water to liquid to make 2 cups. Simmer with remaining ingredients as above. Pour boiling hot over beans and sliced onion rings.

## GAZPACHO ON THE HALF SHELL

*The edible soup bowls are halves of ripe avocados, filled with chopped raw vegetables in the manner of Spanish gazpacho.*

    4 large ripe tomatoes
    1 cucumber
    ¼ cup chopped green pepper
    ¼ cup chopped red onion
    1 small hot red pepper, finely chopped
    3 tablespoons olive oil
    2 teaspoons red wine vinegar
    1 teaspoon salt
       Freshly ground black pepper
    1 clove garlic
    3 avocados
       Fresh lime or lemon juice
       Salad greens

Skin tomatoes and chop finely. Peel and chop cucumber. Mix with green pepper, onion, hot red pepper, olive oil, vinegar, and seasonings. Crush clove of garlic over all. Chill ice cold. Cut avocados into halves lengthwise; remove seed and skin. Sprinkle with fresh lime or lemon juice. Place bowl of "gazpacho" in center of large salad plate; ring around with avocado halves and greens. Heap cold "soup" into avocados. Serve with spoons. Makes six salads.

TRI-COLOR BEAN SLAW

*A sharp contrast of dark and light beans, crisp vegetables, and bacon. Good for outdoor parties.*

    2 cups cooked lima beans
    8 slices bacon
    1 cup canned red kidney beans
    1 large red onion
    2 cups shredded cabbage
    6 thinly sliced red radishes
    ¾ cup mayonnaise
    3 tablespoons vinegar
       Salt and pepper
       Small lettuce leaves

Drain and chill lima beans. Fry bacon crisp. Drain. Drain kidney beans. Slice onion into paper-thin slices and separate into rings. Combine beans, cabbage, onion rings, and radishes. Top with broken up bacon. Mix mayonnaise and vinegar. Pour over salad and toss lightly. Season with salt and pepper if needed. Heap into salad bowl lined with small crisp lettuce leaves. Makes 4 to 5 servings.


## LIMA SALAD, DILL DRESSING

*This is particularly good for barbecues.*

> 4 cups cooked dry lima beans
> 1 clove garlic
> 1 teaspoon salt
> 1 cup sour cream
> 2 tablespoons salad oil
> 3 tablespoons vinegar
> 1 teaspoon sugar
> 2 tablespoons minced parsley
> ½ teaspoon dried dill or 1 tablespoon snipped fresh dill
> Salad greens
> Sliced cucumbers, cherry tomatoes
> Minced parsley

Drain and cool limas. Crush garlic with salt against sides of small bowl. Add rest of dressing ingredients. Pour over limas. Mix gently and chill. Serve in lettuce-lined bowl. Surround with thinly sliced cucumbers and cherry tomatoes. Sprinkle lightly with minced parsley. Makes about 6 servings.


## THE CALIFORNIAN

*Try this novel, light dressing of anchovies and tomato juice on other salads too.*

> 1 tin flat anchovy fillets
> 3 tablespoons olive oil
> 1 tablespoon red wine vinegar
> 1 tablespoon lemon juice
> ¼ cup tomato juice
> 1 teaspoon grated onion

½ teaspoon sugar
  Salt
  Freshly ground pepper
2 soft-ripe avocados
  Salad greens

Drain anchovies; chop fine. Place in jar with next six ingredients. Cover and shake until well blended. Add salt and pepper to taste. Cut avocados into quarters lengthwise. Remove seeds, strip off skin. Lay 2 quarters on crisp lettuce leaves on each plate. Top with anchovy dressing. Decorate with tomato wedges. Makes 4 salads.

*On the half shell:* If you like, serve the dressing in unpeeled avocado halves. Provide a spoon as well as fork.

### ROMAINE WITH ORANGE

Try this refreshing idea on a hot day: Fill a bowl with cold, crisp watercress and romaine. Top with paper-thin slices of sweet oranges, salt, and freshly ground black pepper. Nothing else. Cool juice from sliced oranges provides just enough dressing to accent the romaine—yet lets its own flavor come through. Sometimes we add a few drops of tarragon vinegar.

### TOMATO PLATTER, ITALIAN

Slice big red beefsteak tomatoes onto a large platter. Sprinkle with a few sprigs chopped, fresh sweet basil or crumble about a teaspoon dried sweet basil on top. Squeeze a clove of garlic over all and drizzle generously with olive oil. Chill. Sprinkle with salt and freshly ground black pepper just before serving.

### CHILLED ASPARAGUS WITH MAYONNAISE DIJON

Cook fresh asparagus spears in boiling salted water until just tender. Drain and chill. (Or use top quality canned or frozen spears.) For 6 servings, blend into 1 cup mayonnaise: 2 tablespoons Dijon mustard, 1 teaspoon Worcestershire sauce, ⅛ teaspoon curry powder, 2 tablespoons cream, 2 teaspoons lemon juice. Serve over asparagus.

ARTICHOKES IN TARRAGON ASPIC

*Pale, elegant and cool looking for a special luncheon or buffet party.*

   2 to 3 dozen cooked small artichoke hearts (3 cups)
      2 envelopes unflavored gelatin
   ½ cup cold water
      3 cups boiling hot water
      2 tablespoons dried tarragon leaves
      2 teaspoons salt
      2 tablespoons sugar
      4 tablespoons tarragon wine vinegar
      4 tablespoons lemon juice
      2 tablespoons grated onion
      2 tablespoons finely chopped sweet red pepper or pimiento
      2 tablespoons chopped parsley

Occasionally you can buy small fresh artichokes for hearts. Otherwise, use the canned, or cook frozen ones. Soak gelatin in cold water. Pour 1 cup of the boiling water over crushed tarragon leaves; cover. Let stand until cool. Pour 2 cups boiling water over gelatin. Stir and blend in remaining ingredients. Pour over artichokes. Cover and let stand until tarragon liquid is cool, about 30 minutes. Place 1 dozen artichoke hearts top-side down in 6-cup ring mold. Strain tarragon liquid and add to gelatin. Chill until syrupy. Pour into mold. Chill firm. Unmold on salad platter. Garnish with crisp romaine, quartered hard-cooked eggs. Serve with lemon mayonnaise. Makes about 8 servings.


FRESH MINT JELLY

*Cool as a bunch of mint. Serve with tiny orange rolls and iced tea or coffee.*

      2 tablespoons unflavored gelatin
   ⅔ cup sugar
      2 cups water
   ¼ cup chopped fresh mint leaves
   ½ cup fresh lemon juice
      1 cup pineapple juice
   ¼ cup fresh orange juice
      1 cup drained canned pineapple tidbits
   ½ cup grapefruit sections

1½ cups honeydew and cantaloupe or Persian melon balls
   Watermelon wedges

Stir gelatin, sugar and water together over very low heat until melted. Add mint leaves. Cover and let stand till cool. Strain. Add juices and chill till syrupy. Stir in fruits. Pour into 6-cup mold. Chill firm. Unmold on serving plate and circle with watermelon wedges and sprays of mint leaves. Makes 6 servings.

TRADE WINDS SALAD

*Fresh papayas and pineapple from Hawaii are available practically the year round now in your markets. Use them alone or with fresh berries and melons for glamorous luncheon salads, light desserts or breakfast eye-openers.*

   1 fresh papaya
   1 fresh pineapple
   1 Cranshaw, honeydew or Persian melon
      Strawberries on-the-stem
      Fresh lime wedges
      Assorted dressings

Cut papaya into halves lengthwise and scoop out the tiny black seeds. Pare off rind and cut fruit into fingers. Cut bottom and plume top from pineapple. Cut fruit into halves lengthwise, then pare off the rough outer rind. Cut out hard core; cut pineapple into neat finger-like wedges or spears. Cut melon in halves. Pare off rind and cut into slender slices. Wash and drain unhulled berries. Arrange all in a shallow glass bowl with berries in the center. Serve with plenty of fresh lime wedges or one or more of the dressings below. Makes 6 to 8 servings.

*Salad Dressings*

*Honey-lime:* Shake together in glass jar or bottle, ½ cup honey and ½ cup fresh lime or lemon juice. Or ⅓ cup each honey, lime juice, and sherry wine.

*Chutney cream:* Season 1 cup sour cream with 1 to 2 tablespoons chopped chutney.

*Dessert Dressing*

*Ginger cream:* Stir 2 tablespoons ginger marmalade into 1 cup sour cream. Lime or orange marmalade also may be used.

## PINEAPPLE CHICKEN SALAD

*You may split the almonds or chop them, but they're more interesting left whole.*

> 12 slices canned pineapple
> 3 cups diced cooked chicken
> 2 cups bias-sliced celery
> 2 tablespoons diced pimiento
> 2 tablespoons chopped candied ginger
> ½ cup mayonnaise
> ¼ cup sour cream
> 2 teaspoons lemon juice
> 1 cup salted almonds
>   Salt, pepper, and mace
>   Romaine
>   Preserved kumquats

Chill pineapple. Drain. Combine chicken, celery, pimiento, and ginger. Mix mayonnaise, sour cream, lemon juice. Pour over salad and toss well. Add almonds and season to taste with salt, pepper, a flick of mace. For each salad, stack 2 pineapple slices sandwich-style with chicken salad. Arrange on a serving platter and surround with small, crisp romaine leaves. Top each with a preserved kumquat. Makes 6 servings.

# RELISHES

## SWEDISH PRUNE PICKLES

*The crushed cardamon seeds, so often used in Scandinavian cooking, inspired the name for these spicy prune pickles. Our Swedish friends serve a heaping bowlful for their laden holiday smorgasbord, or sometimes as an accompaniment to rich, crisp-skinned roast goose. We like them in salads too with cool cottage cheese.*

> 12 whole cardamon seeds
> 1 package (2 cups) prunes
> 2 cups apple cider
> ¾ cup good cider vinegar
> 12 whole cloves
>   Dash salt

Peel cardamon seeds and crush with rolling pin. (You should have at least 1½ teaspoons crushed seeds.) Rinse prunes. Combine all ingredients. Simmer gently about 20 minutes. Cool. Pour into quart glass jar. Cover and refrigerate overnight or longer before serving.

### RAISIN MINT RELISH

*Very different—very easy. From Peggy Williams (Mrs. "Deke"). Delicious with barbecued or roasted turkey or chicken, lamb, or pork. Excellent as a sambal to serve with curry.*

Wash and dry a large handful of fresh mint leaves. Rinse and drain 1 cup dark seedless raisins. Grind together and mix with 2 tablespoons India relish. Serve well chilled. Not as good, but you can substitute a few drops mint extract for fresh mint.

### BANANAS ON THE HALF SHELL

*Another interesting curry accompaniment.*

Strip off half the peel of 4 bananas, leaving the bottom half as a shell to hold banana. Slash banana just to the peel into bite-sized chunks. Brush with butter. Dash with dark rum and dark brown sugar. Broil 5 inches from heat until heated through and glazed.

### GINGER HONEY PEACHES

*These are wonderful to serve cold with salads or meat.*

      1 large can cling peach halves
      1-inch piece fresh ginger root, peeled and diced
            or 2 tablespoons chopped candied ginger
      12 whole cloves
      2 strips lemon peel
      ½ cup honey
      ¼ cup lemon juice

Drain peaches. Add spices, lemon peel, and honey to peach syrup. Simmer gently about 5 minutes. Add peaches and lemon juice. Bring just to boil. Pour into refrigerator dish. Cool. Cover and chill overnight or several days.

## MARINATED GREEN CHILES

*Another cold-relish idea! Or serve as a salad over sliced tomatoes, cucumbers, avocados, or salad greens.*

Crush a clove of garlic against sides of small bowl until it practically disappears. Rinse seeds from large (4-ounce) can green chiles. (The seeds contain fire.) Drain. Cut chiles into strips or squares. Place in bowl with garlic, add enough olive oil to cover. Let stand several hours to mellow flavor. Just before serving add about a tablespoon each minced parsley and fresh mint, a few leaves chopped oregano, and red wine vinegar to taste. Mix and season with salt and coarsely ground black pepper.

# Breakfast and Supper Specialties

There are a number of hostesses we know who have become famous for their parties, yet never give a dinner. They specialize in leisurely breakfasts and brunches or little late suppers. The recipes in this chapter are just right for these happy affairs—light in feeling, fun to make and serve, and much less demanding on the cook.

Try the creamy scrambled eggs served in a giant popover shell or make your own custom-seasoned pork sausage for a special brunch, and you'll see what I mean.

POPOVER EGGS

An impressive dish for brunch or a holiday breakfast. Bake the puffy, crisp shell in the shallow round pyrex dish that's 8½ inches across and 2

33

inches deep. Or, if you're serving alfresco, use a heavy skillet the same size and serve right from that.

Popover shell:
    2 eggs, large and fresh
    1 cup milk
    1 tablespoon melted butter or margarine
    1 cup sifted all-purpose flour
    ¼ teaspoon salt

*Popover shell:* Heat oven to 400°. Butter pyrex dish or pan generously, and set in oven to heat. Beat eggs with rotary beater till light. Beat in milk and butter. Stir in, do not beat, flour and salt. Beat lightly or stir till smooth and texture of heavy cream. Pour into sizzling hot baking dish. Bake at 400° 30 minutes. Turn heat down to moderate (350°). Bake about 10 minutes longer to be sure inside is dry. The mixture rises very high at the sides, 5 to 6 inches, then dips into a shell in the center with a little puff in the middle.

Perfect scrambled eggs:
    6 slices lean bacon, diced
    6 eggs
    ⅔ cup cream or evaporated milk
        Salt and freshly ground black pepper
    1 tablespoon butter
    2 tablespoons snipped chives

*Perfect scrambled eggs:* Meanwhile, fry bacon crisp. Drain on paper towels. Beat eggs lightly with wire whisk, blend in cream, salt, and pepper to taste. Pour off bacon drippings from pan, leaving a thin film. Add butter. When bubbly, pour in eggs. Do this about 3 minutes before popover is ready. Turn heat low and cook without stirring about 1 minute. Insert fork at edge and pull cooked part from bottom to center. Do not stir round-and-round, simply lift eggs from bottom with fork in vertical position. This results in creamy eggs in big soft velvety mounds. Sprinkle with bacon and chives. Give a final lift or two. Eggs should still be soft and moist looking. Pile lightly into popover shell. Serve at table. Cut into wedges and lift onto plates with wide spatula. Should serve 6 but we say 4.

34

## FOIL BACON

*Straight, evenly cooked bacon with no attention, no spatter. Ideal for a few slices or a pound.*

Lay bacon slices flat on broiler rack placed over broiler pan. Cover bacon with sheet of foil pressing it firmly but gently in place. Bake in hot oven (400°) 15 minutes, until crisp. Or place in preheated broiler about 4 to 5 inches from heat. Broil 15 to 20 minutes. Drain.

## BROILER PAN EGGS FOR A CROWD

Remove rack and bacon from broiler pan. Pour off any excess drippings but leave a good heavy film on bottom. Carefully drop in eggs. Most modern ranges have pans large enough to hold at least a dozen eggs. Cover with sheet of foil. Bake at 400° 2 to 5 minutes, until whites are set and yolk is filmed over. Season with salt and freshly ground black pepper.

## CUSTOM-MADE PORK SAUSAGE

*Making your own fresh pork sausage is as simple as asking the meat man to grind a chunk of round steak—except in this case he grinds lean pork. You can control how much fat goes into the sausage, and the amount of seasonings. Once you try these, you'll be making them often—particularly nice for holiday breakfasts, and brunches.*

    1 pound lean pork, ground
    ¾ teaspoon salt
    1 teaspoon dried leaf sage
    2 dashes cayenne pepper
    ¼ teaspoon dried thyme
    ½ teaspoon freshly ground black pepper

Have your meat man grind pork once, and rather coarsely. Or, buy a good lean piece of fresh pork leg or shoulder; put through food chopper using medium blade. With your hands or a fork, mix in seasonings. You may use more or less of the herbs and pepper, but we've found this about right to give a delicate flavor and aroma without overpowering the pork. Form into about 6 patties. Fry gently until browned on each side and completely done inside, 12 to 15 minutes.

## STEAK STRIPS AND EGGS

*Sunday morning favorite. Inexpensive flank steak is ideal for this because the meat fibers run lengthwise and you cut across them as you slice it into strips.*

Lay unscored flank steak on board. Cut in half lengthwise so strips will be about 3 inches long. With a very sharp knife placed at a 45° angle, cut crosswise into wafer thin slices. (One steak makes ample strips for 4 to 6 persons.) Heat a large skillet to smoking hot. Drop in about 1 tablespoon butter or margarine—just to coat bottom with a thin film. Quickly lay strips evenly in hot pan, sear about 1 minute. Turn and sear on second side, adding additional butter as needed. The first strips are ready to turn by the time you've gotten them all into the pan. If you let them tarry—they'll be tough and dry. Otherwise, they're juicy and tinged with brown. Sprinkle lightly with salt and freshly ground black pepper. Keep warm. Add additional butter to skillet. Drop in eggs and cook as desired. Serve with hot biscuits or toasted English muffins.


## SWISS EGGS IN A SHELL

*The traditional makings of Swiss eggs. A delicate toast shell makes this dish easier to serve.*

> 6 or 7 thin slices fresh white bread
> Soft butter
> 1½ cups grated natural Swiss cheese
> 6 eggs
> Salt and pepper
> ¾ cup cream
> 4 tablespoons grated Parmesan cheese

Heat oven to 475°. Butter bread on both sides. Fit slices slightly overlapping with points up in 9-inch pyrex pie plate to form a shell. Fill in bottom with last slice. Set in oven to toast lightly for 5 minutes. Reduce heat to 350°. Sprinkle bread with Swiss cheese. Break eggs into shell over cheese. Sprinkle with salt and pepper to taste. Pour cream over eggs. Sprinkle with Parmesan. Bake in moderate oven till eggs are set, about 10 minutes.

CHAFING DISH CHICKEN LIVERS

*This is a good choice for Sunday brunch or holiday drop-in affairs.*

> 2 cups fresh button mushrooms
> 2 cups chicken livers, cut in 1-inch pieces (about 1 pound)
> 5 tablespoons butter
> 1 teaspoon instant minced onion or a tablespoon minced raw
>     onion
>   Salt and freshly ground black pepper
> 3 tablespoons flour
> 2 cups bouillon
> 1 cup cream
> ½ cup dry sherry wine
> 2 tablespoons minced fresh parsley

Clean mushrooms and wipe dry. Cut chicken livers into uniform pieces about size of mushrooms. Heat butter until bubbly, add mushrooms, and cook gently 2 or 3 minutes. Lift from pan. Add livers and minced onion; cook until livers are tinged with brown but still pinkish inside. Lift from pan and sprinkle lightly with salt and pepper. Blend flour into drippings, then smooth in bouillon and cream. Stir over gentle heat until sauce thickens—it should still be light and not too thick. Add sherry, livers, and mushrooms. Add little salt and pepper—but bouillon is usually salty enough to season sauce. Heat until bubbly—but do not boil. Serve in chafing dish or casserole set on candle warmer. Top with parsley. Makes about 8 servings.

CHEESE PANCAKES WITH FRUIT

*The addition of sour cream to the batter of these cottage cheese pan-cakes gives a different texture, and a flavor that's good contrast for fruits.*

> 1 cup fine-curd cottage cheese
> ½ cup sour cream
> ½ cup sifted all-purpose flour
> ½ teaspoon salt
> 1 tablespoon sugar
> ½ teaspoon soda
> 2 eggs, separated
> 1 cup sour cream

37

1 cup crushed pineapple, strawberries, or other tart fruit
Powdered sugar

Press cottage cheese through a fine sieve. Blend with ½ cup sour cream. Sift together flour, salt, sugar, and soda. Beat egg whites till stiff, set aside. With same beater, beat egg yolks, then beat in cheese and sour cream. Stir in flour mixture, then fold in egg whites. This makes a very puffy, spongy batter. If cheese is dry, stir in 2 to 4 tablespoons milk or cream. Drop by spoonful onto hot greased griddle spreading each a little to make cake thinner. When lightly browned, turn and brown second side. Spread each pancake with a dab of sour cream, a spoonful of tart fruit—crushed pineapple, strawberries, tart applesauce. Roll up and sprinkle with powdered sugar. Makes sixteen 3- to 4-inch pancakes.

### C.C.C. BUTTERMILK PANCAKES

*This is the easiest pancake recipe I've ever tried—and the most popular. I've given it to dozens of friends. The secret of the unusual texture is to keep the batter lumpy and turn the cakes before they become dry on top.*

*Here's how they got their name. In our dating days, both my sisters and I served George, my husband, these pancakes often. George named the pancakes C.C.Cs.,—for "Conrads' Concentration Camp" (our name is Conrad). "Once you eat these, you'll never escape," he claimed.*

2 tablespoons butter or margarine
1 cup sifted all-purpose flour
1 teaspoon salt
1 teaspoon soda
1 large egg
1 cup plus 2 tablespoons buttermilk

Heat griddle. Melt butter. Sift flour with salt and soda into a medium-size bowl. Drop in unbeaten egg. Add buttermilk and butter. Stir only until all the flour is moistened—you'll still see a few lumps here and there. Let stand a few minutes. The batter looks thick, spongy, and puffy. Rub griddle with a crumpled piece of greased paper towel. Drop batter by tablespoonsful onto sizzling hot griddle. Spread batter a little with back of spoon so pancakes will be about 3½ inches across and not so thick. Turn as quickly as they brown—before the bubbles break and

38

become dry looking. This is sooner than most recipes say. Brown on second side. Serve at once, with butter and maple syrup or one of the berry syrups such as wild blackberry or boysenberry. Makes 16 to 18 small pancakes.

### BANANA VELVET PANCAKES

*You'll have to try these to know how good and different they are. The banana flavor is intangible, the batter, thick and puffy, not like your usual pancake batter at all.*

    2 small ripe bananas
    2 eggs
  ⅔ cup milk
    2 cups biscuit mix
    2 tablespoons sugar
  ¼ cup melted butter or shortening
      Orange butter or powdered sugar

Mash banana with fork to make ⅔ cup puree. Beat eggs with rotary beater until softly peaked. Stir in milk, banana, biscuit mix, and sugar. Mix lightly leaving a few lumps. Stir in butter. Bake on lightly greased hot griddle, turning when puffy, before all the bubbles break up. Serve with powdered sugar or orange butter. Makes about 20 pancakes.
*Orange butter:* Work about ¾ cup powdered sugar into 2 tablespoons soft butter. Thin with 1 tablespoon orange juice. Add 1 teaspoon grated orange rind.

## TOPPINGS FOR PANCAKES

### WHIPPED BUTTER

*Whipping air into the butter makes it look like twice as much—and gives pancakes a luxurious taste without actually increasing calories. Perfect for hot biscuits and sweet rolls, too!*

Let regular or sweet butter stand at room temperature until softened a bit, 30 minutes or so. In small bowl, whip with mixer until fluffy as air. Serve at once, or refrigerate. Remove chilled whipped butter 30 minutes to 1 hour before using.

*Orange maple butter:* Whip ¼ pound butter or margarine until fluffy. Stir in 2 teaspoons grated orange rind and shaved maple sugar to taste.

*Honey butter whip:* Beat at high speed with electric mixer ¼ cup honey, 2 tablespoons orange juice, dash of salt, 1 egg white. When thickened, slowly stir in 2 tablespoons melted butter or margarine and 2 teaspoons grated orange rind. Especially good on Banana Velvet Pancakes or thin pancakes.

*Blueberry cinnamon sauce:* Add water to the juice of frozen or canned blueberries to make 1 cup. Blend ¼ cup sugar, 2 teaspoons cornstarch, a generous dash of cinnamon. Add to hot blueberry syrup. Cook until thickened. Stir in 1 cup blueberries, 1 tablespoon butter or margarine, and a good squirt of lemon juice. Use fresh blueberries in season. Sweeten to taste.

*Orange cream cheese sauce:* Soften 1 package cream cheese with the juice of 1 large orange. Beat in ½ cup powdered sugar and a few shreds of orange rind. Add more orange juice or powdered sugar if needed as this should be a runny sauce—about the texture of cream.

TOMATO PARMESAN PIE

*Unusual and original as far as I know, this pie is patterned after the famous Quiche Lorraine. It makes an unusual hot vegetable for patio parties, or the main hot dish for luncheon or supper.*

> Pastry for single 9-inch crust
> ¾ cup grated Parmesan cheese
> ¾ cup thinly sliced green onions and tops
> 2 or 3 firm ripe tomatoes
> Flour, salt, and pepper
> ½ cup drained sliced mushrooms or ripe olives
> 2 eggs
> 1 cup heavy cream

Line 9-inch glass pie pan with pastry. Flute edges. Sprinkle bottom with 2 tablespoons Parmesan cheese, half the onions. Slice tomatoes in thick slices (scant ½ inch). Roll in flour and put into the pastry in a single layer. Takes 6 or 7 slices. Sprinkle generously with salt, freshly ground black pepper, half the cheese, the rest of the onions, and the mushrooms. Beat eggs with wire whisk or fork only enough to mix white and yolk; stir in cream. Pour over tomatoes, tilting pan to settle cream to bottom. Sprinkle top with rest of cheese. Bake in hot oven (400°) 35 to 45 minutes, until pastry is browned and pie is set but still a little quivery in very center. Let cool 20 to 30 minutes before cutting. Serve warm. May be cooled completely and reheated. Makes 5 to 6 servings.

## CHIPPED BEEF, BROWN DERBY

*A favorite men's dish served at one of Hollywood's most famous restaurants. The Brown Derby chefs add avocado cut into small balls, but cubes are easier. This recipe is also delicious made with chicken or tuna and served on dainty chive or curry-flavored biscuits.*

> 4 tablespoons butter
> 4 tablespoons flour
> 1 cup milk
> 1 cup cream
>   Dash black pepper
>   Pinch nutmeg
> ¼ pound shredded drief beef
> 1 soft-ripe avocado
> 1 teaspoon lemon juice
> 3 English muffins

Melt butter, blend in flour. Gradually stir in milk and cream. Cook and stir till mixture boils and thickens. Add a little pepper and nutmeg (no salt, please). Stir in beef; simmer 2 minutes. Cut soft-ripe avocado in half, remove seed and skin. Cut in ½-inch dice. Add to beef mixture. Simmer 1 minute longer. Dash with lemon juice. Serve on toasted split English muffins.

## SWISS TOAST VAUDOISE

*Baked cheese sandwiches, after a fashion, but so different—and infinitely better.*

> 1 cup medium cream sauce
> 1 egg yolk

41

Generous dash cayenne pepper
½ teaspoon dry mustard
    Freshly ground black pepper
 1 teaspoon grated onion or 1 teaspoon instant minced onion
¼ cup sliced ripe olives
1½ cups grated, aged Swiss cheese
 6 slices white bread
    White wine for bread

Into warm cream sauce, blend lightly beaten egg yolk, seasonings, onion, olives, and 1 cup cheese. Generously butter a glass baking dish (8 x
12 inches). Dip bread in wine; lay in baking dish. Spread with sauce.
Sprinkle with rest of cheese. Bake in hot oven (450°) until bubbly and
flecked with brown, 15 to 20 minutes. Serve hot to two or three persons.


SHRIMP AND BACON TART

*This is equally good for luncheon, supper, or served in tiny wedges as
an appetizer.*

½ pound bacon
⅓ cup milk
 1 cup rich biscuit mix
    Olive oil
 1 cup cleaned cooked shrimp
 2 thinly sliced green onions
 1 clove garlic, minced
    Thinly sliced tomatoes (about 2)
½ teaspoon crumbled dried sweet basil
    Salt and pepper
    Mozzarella, Monterey Jack or natural Swiss cheese

Dice bacon and fry crisp. Drain. Stir milk into biscuit mix. Roll thin
and fit into 9-inch pie pan. Spread generously with olive oil. Sprinkle
bacon, shrimp, green onions, and garlic on top. Cover with a single layer
of thinly sliced tomatoes. Crumble sweet basil over all. Dash with salt,
a few grindings of black pepper, a few drops of olive oil. Cover with thin
slices Mozzarella or Jack cheese or 1 cup grated Swiss cheese. Bake in
hot oven (400°) 20 to 25 minutes. Cut in wedges.

42

# Fish Can Be a Favorite Dish

There is good reason why epicures of all ages have prized fish as a favorite. It's a delicate food, both in texture and flavor and thus takes kindly to imaginative sauces and embellishments of all kinds. There's nothing wrong with fried fish if it's done well and not overcooked and dry. In fact, it's the perfect way to cook trout, sand dabs and other small fish. But try some of the suggestions in this chapter for poached fish with a light lemon or wine sauce.

The best way to be sure of freshness in your fish products is to buy the specialties your area affords. All kinds are not available fresh in every community, but frozen fish in great variety is distributed everywhere, and the quality in most cases is excellent.

### FISH ON A STICK, INDIAN STYLE

This recipe is the result of our experiments to approximate the fish cooked by the natives around Puerto Vallarta and other tropical villages on Mexico's west coast. There, they slash their beautiful white sierra fish in 4 or 5 places on each side and rub coarse salt into the cuts. Then they impale the whole fish on a stout green stick and anchor it in the sand at an angle over a bed of low coals. When fish is cooked, the stick is thrust into the ground beside you where you can pull off delicious, crisp-skinned bites with your fingers.

The beach provides an ideal setting for this kind of cookout. You can also do it in your backyard, providing you have a spot where you can build a low fire with earth around it to hold sticks or skewers in place. The other essential is fresh whole fish, weighing up to about 2 pounds each. Any small fish that's not too dry will be fine.

Build a wood fire using hickory, or a fruit or nut wood. We started with charcoal then added orange wood. Let burn about an hour to a thick bed of coals. Meanwhile soak several handsful of hickory chips in water 1 hour. Make diagonal slashes at 2-inch intervals down each side of whole cleaned fish. Rub salt into cuts (coarse kosher salt, if possible). Run sharpened sticks or extra long (2½-foot) barbecue skewers through each fish so the tails will be on top when placed over fire. A cork at each end will keep fish from sliding as it warms and cooks.

Press sticks or skewers into ground about a foot from edge of fire tilted at a 45-degree angle over the coals. Add wet hickory chips to fire to produce a good smoke. Replenish occasionally to keep a light smoke going. Add additional wood at edge of fire if needed. Turn fish several times, until skin has a crusty, crisp look and the fish is cooked, but moist. Be prepared for a different texture as the fish is cooked and smoked at the same time. It takes from 1 to 2 hours—depending on the wood used, the fish, and the wind.

If possible, serve outdoors, Indian-style, stuck upright in the ground. Pass plenty of fresh lime or lemon wedges and lots of French bread. Tomatoes and sliced red onions will complete the feast. And beer, of course, in the true Mexican tradition.


SOLE PARMESAN
*This is an elegant but simple recipe that never fails to please. It's better with fresh fish but very, very good with the frozen fillets.*

   1 pound sole fillets

2 tablespoons chopped onion
3 tablespoons butter or margarine
3 tablespoons flour
1 cup milk
½ cup dry white wine
½ cup cream
½ cup grated Parmesan cheese
1 teaspoon lemon juice

Thaw frozen fish by package directions only enough to separate. Lay fish in shallow greased pan that can go into the broiler. Cook onion in butter till golden. Blend in flour, milk, wine. Cook and stir till sauce boils and thickens. Blend in cream and cheese. Add salt and pepper to taste (about 1 teaspoon salt or a little more). Stir in lemon juice. Pour over fish. Sprinkle with more Parmesan cheese. Bake in hot oven (425°) about 15 minutes, until fish flakes easily. But please do not overcook! Run under the broiler a few minutes to glaze with flecks of brown. Serves 3 to 4.

### BROILED SWORDFISH PIQUANT

*This sharply seasoned marinade and basting sauce is a perfect foil for firm textured, full-flavored swordfish.*

4 tablespoons lemon juice
2 teaspoons grated onion
4 tablespoons bottled steak sauce
  Generous pinch curry powder
2 large swordfish steaks (about 1 inch thick)
4 tablespoons melted butter
  Salt and freshly ground pepper
  Minced parsley

Mix lemon juice, onion, steak sauce and curry powder. Pour over swordfish steaks in shallow pan. Marinate 1 hour. Add butter to pan; mix well to coat fish on both sides. Remove fish to greased broiler pan. Sprinkle with salt and pepper. Place in broiler about 3 inches from heat. Broil and baste until browned, 5 to 7 minutes. Turn; sprinkle with salt and pepper. Broil 5 to 8 minutes longer, basting with marinade. Do not overcook. Cut steaks in two and place on 4 warm plates. Heat remaining marinade, add pan juices and pour over steaks. Top with parsley.

*Charcoaled Swordfish:* This is an excellent marinade for barbecued swordfish. Use thicker steaks and double the amount of marinade. Baste constantly during cooking.

## SOLE FLORENTINE

*A fine example of poached fish served with a smooth rich sauce.*

> 1½ cups water
> 1 onion slice or 1 tablespoon instant minced onion
> 2 tablespoons tarragon vinegar
> ½ bay leaf
> ½ teaspoon salt
> 8 large fillets of sole
> 2 10-ounce packages frozen chopped spinach
> 2 cups medium cream sauce (4 tbs. butter, 4 tbs. flour, 2 cups milk, or part cream, salt)
> ½ cup grated Parmesan cheese
> 2 egg yolks
> Freshly ground pepper

In shallow pan or skillet, heat to simmering the water, onion, vinegar, bay leaf, and salt. Fold fillets in half, place in pan and poach gently until white and opaque, about 5 minutes. Drain well. Cook spinach by package directions, omitting salt. Drain. Heat sauce; stir in Parmesan cheese leaving a little out for top of dish. Add a little of the hot sauce to lightly-beaten egg yolks; stir back into remaining sauce. Spread spinach in greased shallow baking dish. Mix in ½ cup of the sauce. With slotted spatula, place fish carefully on spinach. Sprinkle with pepper. Cover with remaining sauce and sprinkle with Parmesan. Place low under broiler until bubbly and glazed with flecks of brown. Makes 8 servings. (If you make this ahead, heat in moderate oven until sauce is hot, then broil to glaze top.)

*Tuna asparagus variation:* Place 2 cups cooked, drained asparagus spears in baking dish. Cover with 2 cans tuna. Top with sauce and Parmesan cheese. Heat in 375° oven until sauce bubbles around edges, about 15 minutes. Run under broiler to glaze lightly.

## BAKED FILLETS ITALIAN

*Fish fillets baked over an aromatic bed of greenery, then covered with sliced tomatoes and a shower of Parmesan cheese.*

2 pounds fish fillets
¾ cup chopped onion (use green onions and tops if available)
½ cup finely chopped celery and tops
½ cup finely chopped parsley
1 teaspoon salt
Black pepper
¼ cup olive or salad oil
2 tomatoes, thinly sliced
⅓ cup grated Parmesan cheese
⅓ cup fine cracker crumbs

Wipe fish with damp paper towels. (If frozen fish is used, defrost just enough to separate.) Preheat oven to 375°. Put onion, celery, and parsley into large shallow baking dish (about 8 x 12 inches). Place fish in overlapping layers on top. Season with salt and pepper. Drizzle with 3 tablespoons oil. Bake at 375° 10 minutes. Cover fish with tomato slices. Sprinkle with salt and pepper, cheese and crumbs mixed. Drizzle rest of oil on top. Bake 30 minutes longer, or until fish is flaky and tomatoes are lightly browned. Makes 6 servings.

## OVEN FRIED FISH

*This easy and simple way to fry fish is known as the Spencer method and is usually suggested for fillets. I've discovered it works beautifully for trout and other small fish. No fuss, no spatter, no fish-frying odor.*

Heat oven to 500°. Generously butter an oblong pyrex baking dish large enough to hold your fish in a single uncrowded layer. On a large sheet of waxed paper or foil, spread a mound of very fine dry bread crumbs or fine corn flakes crumbs. Alongside, pour milk into a shallow dish large enough to dip fish. Season milk with salt. Dip each cleaned fish in milk, then in crumbs to coat evenly. Place flat in buttered dish, fish barely touching each other. Pour melted butter over crumbs. Bake in very hot oven until crisp, golden brown, and tender when pierced gently with a fork.

Takes 12 to 15 minutes. It's usually not necessary to turn fish as the glass dish helps them brown on bottom also. Serve from baking dish with juicy wedges of lemon.

### FROSTED SALMON MOUSSE

*This is an ideal hot weather entrée. Especially effective on a green glass plate decorated with sprays of fresh dill and thin cucumber slices. Make it the day before.*

> 2 pounds canned or cooked salmon*
> 2 envelopes unflavored gelatin
> ½ cup cold water
> 2 teaspoons powdered chicken stock base or 2 chicken bouillon cubes
> 1¼ cups boiling hot water
> 1 teaspoon salt
> 4 tablespoons vinegar
> 4 tablespoons lemon juice
> 2 tablespoons sugar
> 2 teaspoons grated onion
> 2 teaspoons bottled horseradish
> 1⅓ cups mayonnaise

Drain and flake salmon; remove skin and bones. Soften gelatin in ½ cup cold water. Dissolve chicken stock base or bouillon cubes in boiling water; add gelatin and stir till it melts. Blend in salt, vinegar, lemon juice, sugar, onion, and horseradish. Cool until gelatin thickens slightly. Pour thickened gelatin over fish and blend in mayonnaise until smooth. Turn into fish mold and chill firm. Unmold on platter and frost with avocado-dill cream. Serves 10 to 12.

*Avocado-dill cream:* Blend 1 mashed avocado with 1 cup thick sour cream, 1 teaspoon salt, and fresh snipped or dried dill to taste.

*To cook fresh or frozen salmon:* Put 2 inches water in bottom of big kettle or Dutch oven. Add 2 sprigs parsley, 2 slices each lemon and onion, 3 or 4 whole pepper corns. Tie salmon loosely in cheese cloth. When water boils lay salmon on rack or trivet over water. Cover tightly. Steam 10 to 20 minutes (about 10 minutes per pound), or until fish

48

looks opaque and flakes easily, but is still moist. (Salmon steaks will steam tender in 10 minutes.) Turn fish once if it's very thick.

## LOBSTER COCONUT CURRY

*Coconut milk, the unusual spices and coarsely shredded lemon peel add a very special flavor to this curry. Shrimp may be used in place of lobster.*

> 1½ cups flaked or grated coconut
> 2 pounds cooked lobster meat or 6 to 8 frozen rock lobster tails
> 6 tablespoons butter or margarine
> 2 large onions, chopped
> 2 cloves garlic, minced
> 2 tablespoons curry powder
> 1 tablespoon grated fresh ginger root or ½ teaspoon ground ginger
> 3 cardamon seeds, peeled and crushed
> ¼ teaspoon dry mustard
> ½ cup flour
> 2 teaspoons shredded lemon peel
> 3½ cups lobster stock (half may be chicken stock)
> 2 teaspoons salt, or to taste
> ½ cup cream
> 2 tablespoons lemon juice

*Ahead of time:* Make coconut milk by directions below. If lobster tails are used, boil as label directs, adding bay leaf and 4 cloves to water. Drain; save stock. Cut away soft undershell. Remove meat; cut into chunks.

Heat butter in large heavy pan. Add onion and garlic; cook until golden. Sprinkle with curry powder, ginger, crushed cardamon seeds, mustard, and flour. Stir smooth, slowly blend in 1 cup coconut milk, lemon peel and the lobster or chicken stock. Cook and stir over low heat until smooth. Taste; season as needed with salt. Simmer gently 15 to 20 minutes. Stir in lobster, cream, and lemon juice. Heat until bubbling—but do not boil. Makes 6 to 8 servings.

Serve with hot cooked rice. Chopped almonds, sliced green onions, quartered limes, chilled pineapple, and chutney are nice accompaniments.

49

*Coconut milk:* Combine in saucepan 1½ cups flaked coconut and 1⅓ cups milk (or 1 cup packaged grated coconut and 1 cup milk). Simmer over low heat, stirring occasionally until mixture foams—about 2 minutes. Cool slightly and strain, pressing out as much of the creamy coconut pulp as possible. Makes 1 cup.

### BROILED SHRIMP ADRIATIC

*An easy way with a classic Italian shrimp dish! It may also be made in a big frying pan on top of the stove.*

> 2 pounds jumbo raw shrimp, fresh or frozen
> ¼ cup olive oil
> ¼ cup butter
> 1 minced clove garlic
> 2 tablespoons chopped parsley
> Salt and pepper
> Juice of 1 large lemon

Remove shells from shrimp but leave tails intact. Devein and wash in cold water. Dry on paper towels. (No need to defrost frozen shrimp, they handle better while still frozen.) Put oil and butter in shallow pan that can go into broiler. Heat until butter melts. Add garlic and parsley. Sprinkle shrimp with salt and pepper. Swish in oil-butter until well coated. Broil and baste about 4 inches from heat for about 5 minutes. Baste, turn, and broil 5 minutes longer. Remove shrimp to warm serving plate. Add the lemon juice to pan, a little fresh parsley too. Heat and pour over the shrimp. Serve with French rolls so you can soak up every drop of the garlicky lemon sauce. Makes about 4 servings.

### BEER BATTER SHRIMP

*Shrimp fried in a delicate thin batter that's as crisp as a starched lace collar. Pancake mix and beer do the trick! Allow most of the thin batter to drip off before popping the shrimp into boiling hot oil.*

> 1 pound raw shrimp*
> 1 cup packaged pancake mix
> ¾ cup beer
> ¼ teaspoon salt

Deep hot fat
Chinese mustard and catsup

Shell, devein and clean shrimp, leaving tails intact. Combine pancake mix, beer, and salt. Beat with rotary beater until very smooth. Heat deep fat to 370°. Dip shrimp in batter. Hold up to let some of batter drain off. Fry in hot fat 5 to 6 minutes, or until golden and crisp. Drain on absorbent paper. Serve as the Chinese do with small side dishes, each filled with catsup on one side, hot mustard on the other. A curry or mustard flavored mayonnaise also is delicious with these.

*Hot mustard:* Mix water into dry mustard a little at a time until it looks about like cream. Let stand 5 to 10 minutes. Hot—but good!

*You may use pre-shelled shrimp, frozen or fresh. These have usually been cooked before removing shells—so heat fat to 375°; cook 2 to 3 minutes only.

CRAB CRÊPES SCANDIA

*These delicate, stuffed crepes can be made well in advance for a fancy luncheon or buffet. Only one last-minute chore: fold whipped cream into the dill sauce and run under the broiler a few minutes.*

*Crêpes:*
    ½ cup sifted all-purpose flour
    ½ teaspoon salt
    2 eggs
    1 cup milk
    1 tablespoon melted butter

*Filling:*
    1 can frozen cream of shrimp soup (save half of it for sauce)
    1 cup crab meat
    ½ cup sliced ripe olives
    1 tablespoon lemon juice
    Salt, pepper, pinch of nutmeg
    Dill sauce
    1 tablespoon minced parsley

Sift together flour and salt. Beat eggs, flour, and milk until smooth. Set aside ½ hour. Stir in melted, cooled butter. Defrost shrimp soup by placing can under running warm water a few minutes. Mix ½ can with crab meat. Warm over low heat. Add olives and lemon juice. Season to taste with a little salt, pepper, and nutmeg.

Heat small 6-inch skillet. Brush with butter. Remove from heat and add 1½ tablespoons batter, tilting pan quickly to coat bottom evenly. Cook until light brown. Turn and brown lightly. Spread with a spoonful filling; roll up and place in shallow baking dish. Repeat with batter and filling until all is used. Make sauce and pour over crêpes. Broil low in broiler, with low heat until flecked with brown, about 5 minutes. Sprinkle with parsley. Makes 4 to 6 servings.

> *Dill sauce:*
> 2 tablespoons minced onion
> 1 tablespoon butter
> ½ can frozen cream of shrimp soup (left from filling)
> 2 tablespoons milk
> ½ teaspoon dried dill
> 1½ teaspoons lemon juice
> ½ cup heavy cream, whipped

Sauté onion in frothy hot butter until golden. Stir in shrimp soup, milk, and dill. Stir over low heat until bubbly hot. Add lemon juice to whipped cream; fold into sauce.

# Eleven Chickens and a Duck

Chicken has inspired more of the world's great dishes than perhaps any other food. It's not only fine eating in itself, but goes nicely with anything or everything. Considered a luxury in most countries, it has become everyday fare in the United States. That's because it's inexpensive and everyone loves it!

Whether you like your chicken fried crisp and served with a creamy rich gravy, or enhanced with herbs or wine, I hope there will be a recipe here you'll want to try.

### CHICKEN EN COCOTTE

The classic French way with a whole young chicken. Simply butter-roasted in a deep earthenware casserole or French cocotte. It is very tender and succulent.

Rub whole broiler-fryer or roaster (up to 3 pounds) with salt, freshly ground pepper, and 2 to 4 tablespoons soft butter. Place in well-buttered deepish earthenware cocotte or casserole. Roast in moderately hot oven (375°) for 1 to 1½ hours, depending on size. Baste with the buttery pan juices about every 15 minutes. It's worth it. You may need to turn heat up to 400° last 20 minutes or so for a deeper brown. When golden rich brown and tender, remove from oven and let stand at least 15 minutes. (Keep warm.) Both texture and flavor are improved by this as the natural juices sort of settle themselves. To serve, cut into quarters or halves with poultry shears.

*This is the basic recipe.* For dress-up, try this: Add 1 can each drained artichoke hearts and ripe olives to pan sauce. Heat through and place with chicken on hot serving dish.

Rice or noodles are good served with this chicken. Cook them in stock made by simmering neck and giblets in salted water while chicken roasts.

Gravy: Rice and noodles call for sauce or gravy—but keep it on the light, delicate side. Blend about 2 teaspoons flour into pan drippings. Put over direct heat or transfer to a pan that can go over burner. Be sure to get out all the brown crumbles. Slowly stir in ½ cup table cream and ¼ cup sherry or dry white wine, scraping brown up from bottom. Cook and stir until hot and smooth. Add salt, pepper and 1 teaspoon lemon juice. Pour around chicken.

MARIN COUNTY CHICKEN CURRY

*Serve your curry and rice, each in its own chafing dish or casserole, on a brass or bamboo tray, accompanied by fresh pineapple shells and To-matoes Johannesburg. On another tray nearby arrange some or all of the suggested condiments in small bowls with individual serving spoons. (A perfect way to use your collection of souvenir spoons.)*

*Suggested condiments: Mango chutney, diced bananas, chopped crystallized ginger, grated coconut, chopped salted peanuts, and snips of crisp green pepper.*

> 1 (4 to 5 pounds) stewing or roasting chicken*
> 1 sliced onion
>    Handful celery tops

54

8 whole black peppercorns
6 cups water
1 tablespoon salt

*Stewing chicken is less tender, but fatter and makes very flavorful broth. Roasters are meatier, more expensive.
*Day ahead:* In large kettle simmer above ingredients until chicken is tender, 1½ to 2 hours. Cool over night. Skim off fat and save it. Strain stock.

6 tablespoons butter and chicken fat
3 large onions, chopped
2 cloves garlic, minced
1 cup chopped celery
2 to 3 tablespoons curry powder
½ teaspoon ground ginger
1 quart stock from chicken
2 dried red chili peppers, chopped
2 tablespoons chutney
Handful of raisins
1 cup cream
4 tablespoons flour
Juice of half a lemon

*Next day:* In large chicken fryer or Dutch oven heat butter and chicken fat until bubbly. Add vegetables and cook until soft. Mix curry powder and ginger to a paste with a little chicken stock. Blend into stock, then add to vegetables. Stir in peppers, chutney and raisins. Simmer while blending cream into flour. Stir in. Simmer at least 1 hour. Cut chicken from bones in big pieces and add to sauce. Add lemon juice. Heat gently till chicken is hot. Serve with rice and suggested accompaniments. Makes 6 servings.

## FRESH PINEAPPLE SHELLS

Wash and tear away dry outside leaves of ripe pineapples. Split lengthwise through leafy top. Cut fruit out of shell with sharp grapefruit or paring knife. Cut away hard center core; dice fruit into bite-size chunks and put back into shells. Cover with waxed paper and chill.

## TOMATOES JOHANNESBURG

*Friends from South Africa gave us this cool idea for curry.*
Fry 5 or 6 strips lean bacon crisp. Drain and crumble over sliced chilled tomatoes just before serving. Sprinkle lightly with salt and freshly ground black pepper.


## GEORGE'S FRIED CHICKEN

*"Whatever happened to fried chicken?" A stock comment in our house when we're in the throes of working out some fancy chicken recipe. This simple dish—an American classic—is simply great when tenderly, carefully cooked as in the recipe below.*

Buy whole fresh fryers or roasters weighing at least 2½ pounds each. Cut them into pieces at the joints with a sharp knife. Rinse chicken, dry and rub with cut side of lemon. Sprinkle generously with salt and freshly ground black pepper; drop into bag containing ½ cup flour for each chicken. Shake until pieces are coated. Remove and shake off all loose flour.

Meanwhile, heat ½ inch mild salad oil in large heavy skillet or chicken fryer. When oil is sizzling hot, add chicken pieces and 1 tablespoon butter. Overcrowding will prevent an even browning. Cook over medium fire until crisp and a rich golden color. Watch it . . . and add a little butter from time to time if needed. After about 10 to 15 minutes gentle frying, set lid on skillet, slightly ajar, to allow a little steam to form yet browning process to continue. Cook a few minutes. Turn chicken with tongs. Brown slowly on second side; cover again but leave lid ajar. Cook until tender. Fresh, top quality, room-temperature chicken will be ready to eat in about 30 to 45 minutes. Drain on paper towels. It's best served immediately. Since this is not always possible, place it in a shallow baking dish, cover loosely with foil and heat 30 minutes or so in a 300° oven. Uncover last 5 minutes to crisp skin.

Cream gravy: Make it thin! Serve it hot! Drain fat from skillet saving 2 tablespoons. Scrape up crumbs from bottom. Smooth in 2 tablespoons flour. Then slowly add 2 cups milk or part cream. Add any liquid and crumbles from chicken dish. Cook and stir gently until gravy is bubbling hot and texture of smooth cream. Season to taste with salt, pepper, and a pinch of nutmeg.

*Cold chicken:* If that be possible, this is as good or better served cold or at room temperature, next day. A good summer stunt is to fry several on Friday. Keep in the refrigerator for week-end raiders.

## PARTY DRUMSTICKS

*Easier than the traditional fried chicken—spicy and crisp! Wrap the bone ends in a paper frill, heap drumsticks into a basket for informal suppers, patio parties—a brunch.*

Cover chicken fryer drumsticks with buttermilk. Marinate several hours or overnight. Drain and pat dry. Rub with salt and freshly ground black pepper. Dip in melted butter to which you've added crushed clove garlic, a little crumbled leaf sage, minced parsley, plenty of paprika. Then roll drumsticks in mixture of equal parts flour and grated Parmesan cheese. Place uncrowded in buttered shallow glass dish. Drizzle with a little melted butter. Bake in 375° (moderately hot) oven about 1 hour, or until very crisp. Usually not necessary to turn.

## SESAME CHICKEN

*Fried in the oven from start to finish—this is an easy dish for parties and guest dinners.*

    1 frying chicken, disjointed
      Salt, pepper, flour
    1 teaspoon paprika
    2 tablespoons butter
    2 tablespoons salad oil
    2 tablespoons sesame seeds
    ½ cup dry white table wine
    ¼ cup finely chopped green onions or scallions

Sprinkle chicken with salt and pepper to your taste. Shake in a paper bag containing flour mixed with paprika. Shake off excess flour. Melt butter in shallow glass baking dish, about 12 x 8 inches. Add oil. Turn chicken in mixed butter and oil till coated all over. Lay pieces in single flat layer, skin side down. Sprinkle with half the sesame seed. Bake in hot oven (400°) 30 minutes. Turn chicken skin side up. Pour wine and onion over it. Sprinkle with rest of sesame seed. Cook at 375° 45 minutes longer, or until chicken is golden brown and tender. Baste occasionally with pan sauce. Makes 4 servings.

*Gravy fans:* Remove chicken. Pour drippings into pan and blend with a little flour to thicken. Add more wine, if you like, and cream and chicken stock ad lib. Cook and stir over low heat till it's the texture you like.


EASY CHICKEN PIE

*If you dislike boiling a chicken for chicken pie, here's the answer. Use meaty fryer parts cooked this way.*

> 2 packages frozen chicken parts or about 12 meaty pieces fresh chicken fryer
> 4 ounces chicken livers (or ½ package frozen)
>   Salt and pepper
> 2 cans cream of chicken soup
> 1 cup half-and-half or rich milk
> 1 small can whole onions, drained
> 1 can mushrooms
> 1 cup cooked peas or artichoke hearts
> 2 cups biscuit mix
> 2 tablespoons butter, melted
> 1 teaspoon poppy seeds

Thaw frozen chicken and liver by package directions. Sprinkle with salt and freshly ground pepper. Put in large covered baking dish (3½-quart size or 2 smaller ones). Cover with chicken soup and milk blended together. Cover and cook in moderate oven (350°) until tender, about 1½ hours. Gently stir in onions, mushrooms, and artichoke hearts. Raise temperature to 425°. Make up biscuit dough. Roll and cut with 2-inch cutter. Dip each biscuit in melted butter. Lay in ring on top of chicken, overlapping each biscuit slightly. Sprinkle with poppy seeds. Bake 15 to 20 minutes until biscuits are browned and done underneath. Makes 6 to 8 servings.

## CHICKEN NANTUCKET

*Here's a do-ahead, party dish to make when you have leftover white meat of turkey or chicken. Otherwise, buy and cook chicken breasts. Cover chicken slices with poached scallops and this heavenly sauce.*

> 1 pound scallops
> ½ cup dry white wine
> 2 tablespoons finely chopped onion
> 3 tablespoons butter or margarine
> 3 tablespoons flour
> ½ cup milk
>    Salt, pepper, nutmeg
> ½ cup cream
> ½ cup grated Swiss Gruyère cheese
> 8 slices cooked breast of chicken
> ¼ cup grated Parmesan cheese

Poach scallops in simmering wine 2 to 3 minutes only (do not boil, do not overcook). Remove from liquid. Cook onion in melted butter briefly. Smooth in flour. To scallop-wine liquid add enough milk to make 1 cup. Blend into butter. Cook and stir till sauce boils and thickens. Season with salt, pepper, a dash of nutmeg. Stir in cream, Gruyère cheese. Lay chicken in shallow greased baking dish. Cover with scallops cut in quarters. Pour sauce on top and sprinkle with Parmesan. Run under broiler to heat through and glaze lightly with flecks of brown. Makes 4 servings.

*To make ahead:* Prepare chicken and scallops. Place in dish. Make sauce. A few minutes before serving, heat sauce and pour over scallops. Heat through and glaze as above.

## SUPRÊMES OF CHICKEN, CHAUD-FROID

*A distinguished recipe for elegant summer dinners, or for luncheon any season.*

*The three distinct steps of the recipe, when looked at separately, are simple and familiar procedures.*

*First, breasts of chicken are cooked, cooled, and removed from bone. Next, they're mantled in a satiny white sauce called chaud-froid—liter-*

ally a cold, hot sauce. Last, when the sauce is set, it's glazed with a thin film of clear aspic flavored with lemon and tarragon.

>Spray of parsley, slice of onion, spiral of lemon peel
>1 teaspoon salt
>1 cup water or chicken stock
>2 whole breasts of chicken fryers
>2 tablespoons butter
>2 tablespoons flour
>Dash of nutmeg, white (or black) pepper
>2 egg yolks
>½ cup cream
>1½ teaspoons unflavored gelatin
>½ teaspoon dried tarragon leaves, crushed
>2 teaspoons lemon juice
>Decorations: sliced ripe olives, pimiento strips, watercress leaves

*To cook chicken breasts:* Put parsley, onion, salt, and lemon peel in bottom of 3-quart saucepan with water or chicken stock. Lay chicken, skin up, on a rack or trivet, over water. Cover pan and steam tender, about 45 minutes. Remove chicken to cool. Strain stock. Add milk if needed to make 1 cup liquid.

*Chaud-froid sauce:* Melt butter in saucepan, blend in flour with French wire whisk or spoon. Slowly whisk in the 1 cup stock. Stir over low heat until it bubbles and thickens. Season with dash (less than 1/16 teaspoon) of nutmeg, pepper, and a little extra salt if needed. Taste. With whisk, stir egg yolks and cream together. Add a little hot sauce. Stir back into sauce pan. Cook and stir about ½ minute longer. Remove from heat. Soften gelatin in 2 tablespoons cold water. Stir 1 tablespoon of this into hot sauce. Cool slightly.

Pull skin from chicken breasts. Slip point of knife between meat and bone, lift meat off each breast in 2 fillets. Place on serving platter. French recipes usually say trim into neat ovals but the chicken breast has a pretty shape and is too precious to waste. I simply trim off any taggy pieces and put them under the breast. Pour slightly cooled chaud-froid sauce over chicken to mantle completely. Some will run down into platter, but spoon it back to keep shapes neat as it cools and sets. Cool.

Glaze: Pour ½ cup boiling water over tarragon leaves. Cool covered. Strain. Heat and stir in the remaining softened gelatin and lemon juice. Cool until syrupy. Decorate tops of chicken as you like with sliced ripe olives, pimiento strips, or watercress leaves. Spoon glaze over tops in shiny film; cool until set. Makes 4 servings. May be doubled easily.

## CHICKEN BREASTS, PROSCIUTTO

*Boned chicken breasts—or suprêmes de volaille, to use the authentic French name of these delicacies—are fun to cook and make a very impressive party dish. The secret seems to lie in cooking them gently only until tender and brown, as prolonged heat dries them out and makes the delicate white meat tough. These are stuffed with prosciutto, though I sometimes make the same recipe with canned pâté de foie gras. Serve the breasts on a bed of fine green noodles with broiled tomato halves.*

> 4 boned, skinned chicken breasts (cut from 2 fryers)
>   Lemon juice, salt and pepper
> 4 slices prosciutto (Italian ham)
>   Flour
> 6 tablespoons butter
> 1 finely chopped green onion
> ¼ cup finely chopped mushrooms
> ¼ cup dry vermouth
> 1¼ cups consommé or bouillon
>   3 tablespoons heavy cream
>   1 egg yolk
>   1 tablespoon lemon juice

Flatten breasts slightly; brush with lemon juice and season very lightly with salt and pepper. Cover each with a thin slice of prosciutto to fit. Press down firmly, then fold over pocketbook-style. Press edges together and fasten with picks. Dust lightly with flour. Melt butter over very low heat and discard white sediment at bottom. Heat 4 tablespoons in heavy skillet. Cook chicken gently until a rich golden brown and cooked through, about 5 to 6 minutes on each side. Transfer to warm serving dish; dot with butter and cover loosely. Heat in moderate oven 10 minutes or so while you make sauce.

*Sauce:* Sauté onion and mushrooms in rest of butter a few minutes. Add vermouth and consommé; boil about 5 minutes to reduce liquid slightly. Beat cream into egg yolk. Off heat, stir a little of hot liquid into yolk, then stir back into pan. Add lemon juice; heat a second, then remove from fire. Put spoonful on each suprême. Serve rest of sauce in separate sauceboat. 4 servings.

*Boned chicken breasts:* These are not difficult to do. Cut whole breasts in two lengthwise with heavy knife or poultry shears. Insert a small, sharp-pointed knife between meat and breast bone. With other hand, gently pull and strip meat away pushing it with the knife point.

### HERB BARBECUE CHICKEN

*The secret of good barbecued chicken is to keep it moist—by marinating ahead of time and by basting all during cooking. However, if you have a motorized spit and wire basket, the chicken bastes itself as it turns and thus retains all its juices. Less work for you.*

>      2 broiler-fryer chickens
>      1 lemon
>        Salt, coarsely ground black pepper
>      1 clove garlic, crushed
>    ½ cup dry white table wine
>      2 tablespoons red wine vinegar
>      1 tablespoon sugar
>      1 cup salad oil (we like half olive—half corn oil)
>  2 or 3 sprays each of fresh rosemary, thyme, and marjoram,
>            finely chopped (or 1 teaspoon each of dried)
>  1 or 2 leaves fresh sage (or pinch of dried)

With poultry shears or heavy knife cut chicken into quarters leaving the breast and wing in one part, the leg and thigh in the other. Rinse, pat dry with paper towels. Rub all over, inside and out, with cut lemon, squeezing a little of the juice out as you rub. Sprinkle both sides with salt and freshly ground black pepper. Lay skin side down in shallow glass dish. Mix rest of ingredients and pour over chicken. Turn frequently and let chicken stand in this all afternoon, at least; overnight is better. To grill over charcoal, rake coals to back of fire box. Make a long rectangular pan (about 6 inches wide) of heavy-duty foil. Place in front of coals to catch the grease drippings that cause the coals to flame up. Place chicken in wire basket, clamp into place and put on spit over coals.* Cook 45 minutes to 1 hour. Stop motor occasionally and brush chicken with the marinade. The chicken should be beautifully brown, and fragrant with herbs, juicy but done all the way through.

*If you don't have a motorized spit and basket, lay marinated chicken, skin side up, over coals first. This seals the cut side so the juices are not lost when you turn the pieces over to brown and crisp the skin. Brush constantly with marinade.

### CURRY GLAZED CHARCOAL CHICKEN

*This may seem like a lot of seasoning, but try it! The results will speak for themselves.*

> 2 broiler-fryer chickens, split into halves
> Chinese seasoning powder*
> 1 crushed clove garlic
> 3 teaspoons curry powder
> Salt and freshly ground black pepper
> ¼ cup honey
> ¼ cup Worcestershire sauce
> ¼ cup red wine vinegar
> 1 teaspoon dry mustard
> ¼ cup salad oil
> ¼ cup melted butter

Rub cleaned chicken halves with Chinese seasoning powder, garlic, and the curry powder. Sprinkle with salt and freshly ground black pepper. Combine rest of ingredients except butter. Pour over chicken in non-metallic dish. Let stand several hours or overnight. Turn occasionally. Place chicken over coals, skin side up. Cook slowly until tender and glazed, 45 minutes to 1 hour. (Both honey and butter tend to brown quickly so cook the chickens slowly—at least 8 inches from coals.) Turn frequently, and baste with the marinade frequently—it's worth the effort. Add butter to marinade last half hour of cooking. (We usually cook this in a wire basket that can turn on the motorized spit. Less attention and basting is needed—and about 15 to 25 minutes extra time allowed.)

*Available at most grocers who carry Chinese items. MSG powder may be substituted.

### GLAZED DUCKLING QUARTERS

*Quartered and oven roasted, these are succulent and beautifully glazed. Much easier to serve and less fat than roast duckling.*

> 1 Long Island duckling, fresh or frozen
> ¼ cup orange juice
> ¼ cup port wine
>   Salt to taste
> 2 teaspoons grated onion
> 2 tablespoons grated orange rind
> 2 tablespoons honey
> 1 teaspoon Kitchen Bouquet

Defrost the frozen duckling by leaving in refrigerator overnight. With poultry shears or heavy scissors, remove wing tips, if they aren't already off, and neck. Cut through skin, flesh, and bone from vent to neck very close to either side of the breastbone. It isn't half as hard as it sounds. You can do it with a sharp knife but shears are easier. The breast is now split in two. Now turn duckling over and split the back in two, cutting close to one side of the backbone. Make a cut close along the other side of the backbone and remove it. Cut each half in two just above the thigh.

Mix together orange juice, wine, salt, onion, and 1 tablespoon of the orange rind. Pour over duckling and let stand 30 minutes. Place pieces, skin side up on rack in shallow roasting pan. Roast in slow oven (325°) until tender, about 1 to 1½ hours. Baste occasionally with marinade. Fifteen minutes before removing from the oven, mix last tablespoon orange rind with honey and Kitchen Bouquet. Brush over duckling and cook until it is glazed. Makes 4 servings.

# Meat as the Star

Once you have chosen the meat for your meal the supporting dishes—
the vegetables and other accompaniments—are more easily decided.

For instance, rich pork needs robust companions like broccoli or red
cabbage. It also lends itself well to stuffings such as the unusual wheat
pilaf given later in this chapter. Mint or bright peas are often suggested
for lamb, but have you ever thought of cooking it with artichokes in the
Mediterranean style? You'll find a recipe here that tells how to do it
with thrifty lamb shanks. The delicate flavor of veal seems to call for a
rich, well-seasoned sauce and a contrasting, delicate vegetable or the
sharp accent of fresh lemon I've given it in Fritta Piccata. And beef
stew, homey and American, gains a subtle new flavor and style when
you add herbs and a little red wine.

65

RED CHECK STEW

*An honest, American beef stew with a French touch in the delicate herb seasoning and the addition of good red wine.*

    ¼ pound salt pork, diced
    2 onions, chopped
    2 pounds stewing beef, cut up
    1 teaspoon sugar
    Flour
    ¾ teaspoon salt
    ¼ teaspoon thyme
    Freshly ground black pepper
    1½ cups hot water
    ½ cup dry red wine
  6 or 8 small carrots
    4 small potatoes
    8 small onions

Fry salt pork in heavy pan or Dutch oven till browned. Pour off any more than 2 tablespoons of drippings. Add chopped onion. Stir and fry till soft looking. Push to side of pan, drop in beef. Cook till richly browned, sprinkling with the sugar and a light dusting of flour as it cooks. Sprinkle with salt, thyme, pepper, then add hot water and wine. Cover tightly and simmer very, very gently about 1½ hours. Add additional hot water and/or wine if it seems needed—but don't make it too soupy. Clean and pare or scrape vegetables. Cut potatoes and carrots in half, leave onions whole. Drop into stew. Cook 45 minutes longer or until vegetables are tender. Shake together in a small jar 1½ tablespoons flour and ½ cup cold water. Blend into stew. Cook until gravy thickens slightly and the flour is completely cooked. Four to six servings.

OVEN BEEF BRISKET

*Fresh brisket so often boiled and served with horseradish sauce is much more delicious cooked this way. It shrinks considerably less, too. Long slow baking is the secret.*

    3 pounds boneless beef brisket
    Salt and pepper

66

1 small onion, chopped
1 stalk of celery, chopped
½ bay leaf

Sprinkle meat with salt and pepper to taste. Put onion and celery on bottom of 2-quart casserole. Lay brisket on top; add bay leaf. *No water.* Cover and bake in moderate oven (350°) 3½ hours or until meat is melting tender. Slice thin and serve with steamed whole potatoes and hot cream mustard.

*To make a complete and easy oven dinner*, put small whole potatoes in a covered casserole with ½ cup boiling water. Prepare a package of gingerbread mix. Cook both in oven at the same temperature while the brisket cooks last hour.

*Hot cream mustard:* Blend cold water into 1 tablespoon dry mustard until it is consistency of heavy cream. Let stand 15 to 20 minutes. Mix with ½ cup sour cream, a little vinegar and salt to taste.

### FLANK STEAK TERIYAKI

*A steak that won't "bust the budget." For tender, juicy flank steak cook very, very briefly. Then slice on a slant, almost as thin as bacon.*

1 flank steak, unscored (about 1½ pounds)
¼ cup soy sauce
¼ cup sherry wine or sake
¼ cup salad oil
1 teaspoon grated fresh ginger (or 2 teaspoons minced preserved ginger)
1 clove garlic, crushed
1 teaspoon sugar (omit if you use preserved ginger)

Cut steak lengthwise into 2 longish steaks. Trim off any fat or membrane. Do not score. Mix remaining ingredients in a shallow glass pan. Marinate steaks in mixture at least 1 hour. Turn frequently. Lay steaks on grate over hot coals about 2 inches from heat. Or place in broiler close to heat. Grill quickly, 4 to 5 minutes on each side, basting with marinade. Transfer steaks to board, preferably one with a well to catch the juices. With a sharp carving knife or ham slicer cut on a slant into

67

thin slices, across the grain of the meat. With a spatula, scoop up slices and place on four warm plates. Spoon any juices over steak slices. Serve with thick slices French bread and a tossed green salad to four.

## MOTHER BATEMAN'S CORNISH PASTIES

*The Cornish pasty—pronounced like past, not paste—is a kind of meat pie, but infinitely better. My husband's mother came from a Cornish family and has taught me these tricks:*

*1) Use part kidney suet in the pastry when possible, also some in the filling. 2) Meat and vegetables must be put in raw and cooked slowly in the rich crust. 3) In order to end up with a fat meaty pie, not all pastry, literally pack the filling on half the dough as you fold the other half over it like a turnover. I find smaller, individual pasties, baked two nested together in a pie pan, are much easier to handle than the traditional big kind.*

> 3-cup recipe for rich pie dough
> 1½ pounds round steak
> 4 medium potatoes
> 1½ cups chopped onion
> 1½ teaspoons salt
> Black pepper
> 4 tablespoons chopped parsley
> 4 tablespoons kidney suet or butter

Make and chill pastry. Cut round steak into ½-inch cubes. Pare potatoes, cut into very thin slices, then dice. Mix meat, potatoes, onion. Season with salt and lots of black pepper. Divide pastry into 4 parts; roll each into 9-inch circle. Lay one pastry circle in 8-inch pie pan. Heap one-fourth of filling on half of it. Sprinkle with parsley, dot with butter or diced suet. Dampen edges of pastry with water. Very carefully fold pastry over filling, pushing the filling up and mounding it so that the pastry is half-moon shaped and just fills half the pie pan. Crimp edges together to seal just as you do a pie. Repeat with next pastry and filling. Assemble it on the bread board, then with pancake turner lift and fit into pie pan beside first pasty. Make remaining two pasties the same. Prick top with fork. Bake in hot oven (400°) about 15 minutes. Reduce heat to 350° and bake 45 minutes to an hour longer. Makes 4 pasties.

## SWEDISH MEAT BALLS

*Airy, tender, and gently spiced! For cocktail nibbles, heat without sauce and serve from chafing dish with picks. For an informal supper or buffet, serve in one of the delicious sauces along with flaky, hot rice.*

> 1 pound ground round steak
> ⅓ pound ground veal
> ⅓ pound ground fresh pork
> 1 cup milk
> 1½ cups soft bread crumbs
> ½ cup finely minced onion
> 2 tablespoons butter or margarine
> 2 teaspoons salt
> ¼ teaspoon nutmeg
> ¼ teaspoon allspice
> ¼ teaspoon ground cardamon
> Black pepper to taste
> 2 eggs, slightly beaten
> 4 tablespoons butter for frying

Ask your meat man to grind meats together. Otherwise, mix thoroughly with your hands until well blended. Pour milk over bread to soak. Cook onion in butter, a few minutes, until soft. Combine all ingredients except butter for frying. Mix well. (The mixture is soft and hard to handle —but that's what makes the meat balls so airy and light.) With wet hands, form into about 4½ dozen small meat balls. If possible, refrigerate overnight to mellow flavors; remove from refrigerator to "warm up" a few minutes before frying. Dust lightly with flour. In large skillet, heat half your butter until bubbly. Drop in balls, a few at a time. Brown slowly on all sides, shaking pan frequently to keep balls round. Add more butter and meat balls until all are browned, removing finished ones to casserole. Heat as is or in one of the sauces for 30 minutes. Makes 4½ dozen meat balls.

## SAUCES FOR SWEDISH MEAT BALLS

*Swedish cream sauce:* Into pan drippings, stir 2 tablespoons flour. Slowly blend in 1 cup consommé, 1½ cups cream. Cook and stir until thickened—but still on the thinnish side. Season to taste with salt and pepper, and ½ teaspoon caraway seeds, if you like.

*Red wine sauce:* Into pan drippings, stir 3 tablespoons flour. Gradually blend in 1 cup bouillon, 1 cup water, and 1 cup dry red wine such as Burgundy, claret or zinfandel. Cook and stir a few minutes until slightly thickened.

### NORTH ITALY MEAT BALLS

*Chopped spinach and lots of eggs account for the unusual light texture and different flavor of these meat balls.*

> 1 10-ounce package frozen chopped spinach
> 3 eggs
> 2 slices fresh bread
> 3 tablespoons grated Parmesan cheese
> 1 small onion, grated
> 1 teaspoon salt
> 1 clove garlic, crushed
>   Coarsely ground black pepper
> 1 pound ground lean beef
> ¼ pound bulk pork sausage
> 2 tablespoons olive oil

Cook spinach quickly; drain. Beat eggs, add bread, cheese, onion, spinach, salt, garlic, and pepper to taste. Add meats and mix thoroughly with hands. Moisten hands and form into 30 small balls. This is a very soft mixture—that's what makes meat balls so tender. Roll lightly in flour. Refrigerate overnight to mellow the flavors. . . . Or fry at once in hot olive oil until browned on all sides, shaking pan frequently to keep balls round. Transfer to covered dish. Finish cooking "as is" or in a sauce, about 30 minutes in moderate oven. If desired, you may refrigerate these after browning, then heat next day as described above.

*Good sauces for these meat balls:* Paisano Spaghetti Sauce (see index), or red wine sauce under Swedish Meat Balls.

### PERFECT STUFFED PEPPERS

*For years my husband asked for stuffed bell peppers but was always disappointed with my efforts. The filling was too solid and compact, the* peppers had lost their fresh garden taste. After talking with some old-timers and doing a little improvising, I finally found a recipe that's just right. I'm sure the nutty flavor and light feathery texture of the new quick brown rice adds much to its goodness.

        ¾ cup quick brown rice, to be cooked
        5 large green peppers
        1 large onion, finely chopped
        1 pound ground lean chuck
    2½ cups canned tomatoes
        2 eggs
            Salt, pepper, seasoned salt
    2 to 3 strips bacon, halved

Cook rice, covered, in 1¼ cups boiling salted water for 15 minutes. Cut a thin slice from top of peppers. Rinse out seeds and drop peppers into boiling water for 3 minutes only. Don't let them get soft. Drain and set upright in deepish baking dish. Mix half the onion, all the beef, and half the tomatoes. Stir in eggs, beaten lightly with a fork. Season with 1 teaspoon salt, pepper, and seasoned salt to your liking. Lightly mix in cooked rice. Pile into peppers. Top each pepper with a piece of bacon. Put rest of tomatoes and chopped onion in dish around peppers. Cover casserole. Bake in hot oven (400°) about 45 minutes. Uncover and bake about 15 minutes longer, to brown top and crisp bacon. Makes 5 servings.

### SAN FRANCISCO HAMBURGERS

*Patterned after those jumbos served at several San Francisco restaurants, this is my idea of a perfect hamburger. Good ground beef enlivened with red wine and onion, pan-fried in olive oil and served inside a quartered loaf of French bread.*

        2 pounds ground lean beef
        1 teaspoon salt
    ½ teaspoon seasoned salt
            Coarse black pepper
    ½ cup chopped sweet red onion
    ½ cup dry red wine
        1 loaf sour dough French bread

71

Soft butter
1 split clove garlic, if desired
Olive oil

Sprinkle beef with salt, seasoned salt, pepper and onion on cutting board. Gradually add 6 tablespoons wine, cutting through meat with knife to work in seasonings without too much handling. Form meat into 4 thick jumbo patties. Cut French loaf into 4 big "sandwich buns" or chunks. Split each and pull out some of the soft insides to make the "bun" less heavy. Spread with butter. Brush with cut clove garlic if you like. Cook meat to desired doneness in a hot skillet with 1 or 2 teaspoons olive oil. Add the 2 tablespoons wine towards the last, spoon over meat. Hurry into French buns, juice and all. Enjoy with a glass of red wine and a platter of sliced beefsteak tomatoes.

### PORK CHOPS WITH WHEAT PILAF

*Baked double-decker style with stuffing between. Less expensive and much easier than fussing with a pocket in thick chops.*

2 tablespoons butter or margarine
1 cup coarse cracked wheat
½ cup chopped onion
1¾ cups consommé or chicken stock
¾ teaspoon salt
8 lean pork chops
Salt and pepper
1 cup chopped celery
1 cup sliced mushrooms (fresh or canned)
¼ cup chopped parsley
½ teaspoon allspice
½ teaspoon grated orange rind

In heavy pan with tight-fitting lid, heat butter until bubbly. Add cracked wheat and onion. Stir over medium heat until golden. Add consommé and salt. Cover tightly; simmer 15 to 20 minutes, until liquid is absorbed. Meanwhile, season chops with salt and pepper. Brown lightly on each side. Save pan drippings to use later. Place 4 chops in greased baking dish. Stir rest of ingredients into pilaf. Cover each chop in dish with big spoonful pilaf; top with second chop. Secure together with picks to look like 4 thick stuffed chops. (Fill in dish with rest of pilaf or heat it separately in small casserole.) Cover chops and bake in moderate oven (350°) 1 hour. Uncover and pour pan drippings over top. Bake uncovered 30 minutes longer, or until very tender and richly browned. Makes 4 big servings.

## PORK CHOPS NORMANDY

*A French way with pork chops . . . baked with apples, white wine and cream.*

> 6 lean pork chops
> Salt and pepper
> ¼ teaspoon mace
> 2 teaspoons grated orange rind
> 2 tablespoons butter or margarine
> 4 apples (Jonathans or Gravensteins are delicious here)
> ⅓ cup dry white wine (Chablis, Sauterne)
> ¾ cup cream

Sprinkle chops generously with salt and pepper. Rub in mace and orange rind. Brown lightly in 1 tablespoon of the butter. Spread rest of butter in 2-quart casserole. Peel, core, and cut apples into eighths. Put into casserole, top with chops and wine. Bake in moderate oven (350°) 35 to 40 minutes, until most of wine has evaporated and cooked into meat. Baste occasionally. Pour cream into dish around apples. Cook about 30 minutes longer, until chops are tender. Makes 4 to 6 servings.

## HOLIDAY HAM

*Ham with an honest smoked flavor—and not tenderized to death—is still available. And worth looking for! (I'm not referring to the wonderful, but very expensive, non-tenderized, country smoked hams of Virginia, Tennessee, etc.) Cook it by the recipe below and serve cold or at room temperature, in elegant paper-thin slices. A regal dish, and altogether different from the usual heavy slice.*

Put ham in deepish pan—an old-fashioned roaster is ideal. Add 2 tablespoons mixed pickling spices and 2 to 3 cups port wine—should be at least 1 inch deep. Bake in slow oven (325°) several hours. Follow directions printed on ham wrapper, or allow 25 minutes per pound. Baste occasionally. Remove from oven and pour pan liquids into glass container so you can see the fat layer and skim it off. Pour liquid back over ham; baste frequently until it cools completely. Serve "as is" or glaze.

*Ginger glaze:* Score fat of ham in neat diamonds. Spread with 1 cup ginger marmalade (or orange). Add a few spoonsful of the wine mixture to pan. Bake at 400°, basting frequently, until glazed. Takes about 30 minutes.

*Currant jelly glaze:* Melt ¼ cup red currant jelly enough to mix with ½ cup brown sugar, 1 tablespoon dry mustard, 2 tablespoons of wine mixture. Spread on scored ham. Bake and baste at 400° until glazed, about 30 minutes. For a sauce, add ¼ cup each currant jelly and brown sugar to the remaining wine mixture. Bring to a boil. Thicken slightly with 1 tablespoon cornstarch moistened in a little cold water. Serve hot.

### MEDITERRANEAN LAMB SHANKS

*Little-used lamb shanks achieve true distinction with sunny Latin seasonings and artichoke hearts.*

>     4 meaty lamb shanks
>     2 tablespoons lemon juice
>       Salt and freshly ground pepper
>     2 tablespoons olive oil
>     ½ teaspoon dried oregano
>     1 clove garlic, minced
>     1 onion, quartered
>     1 package frozen artichoke hearts or 2 fresh artichokes
>     2 green bell peppers, quartered
>     1 cup hot bouillon (use part dry white wine, if you like)

Ask the butcher not to crack joints of the shanks—otherwise they lose their neat little "drumstick" shapes. Rub shanks all over with part of the lemon juice. Season with salt and pepper. Brown in olive oil and transfer to casserole. Sprinkle with crushed oregano and garlic, rest of the lemon juice and the olive oil drippings. Add onion. Cover and bake in slow oven (300°) about 2½ hours, or until very tender. (That's right, no moisture is added for the baking.) Add frozen artichokes and green pepper, stirring around to coat with pan juices. Salt lightly. Add

74

hot bouillon. Cover and bake at 350° 20 to 30 minutes, until vegetables are just-cooked. Makes 4 servings.

*Gravy:* Pour off pan drippings into small pan. Thicken with 1 tablespoon cornstarch mixed smooth with ¼ cup cold water. Serve very hot in small bowl.

*If you use fresh artichokes:* Pull off about 2 layers of outside leaves and cut off top one-third of artichoke. Quarter artichokes, lengthwise. With tip of spoon scoop out fuzzy choke in center. All that's left now is edible. Rinse and add to lamb shanks with bouillon. Season with salt. Cover and bake at 350° 30 minutes. Add green pepper; cook 20 to 30 minutes longer.

## LAMB RIBS WITH SAUERKRAUT

*There are approximately 3 or 4 good bites per riblet, so allow about one pound per person. Breast of lamb may be used but it's fatter and more wasteful.*

> 4 pounds lamb riblets
> Salt
> Coarse cracked pepper
> 3½ cups (1 can) sauerkraut
> 1 chopped onion
> 2 red apples
> 2 teaspoons dill seeds
> 5 tablespoons brown sugar

Sprinkle lamb with salt and pepper. Place on rack of roasting pan. Cook at 350° 1 hour. Drain off fat. Put sauerkraut, onion, and unpeeled apples, cut into wedges, in shallow greased baking dish. Mix in dill seeds. Sprinkle with brown sugar. Top with riblets. Cook 1 hour, or until brown and crisp. Makes about 4 servings.

## CHARCOALED LAMB ARABIC

*A spectacular way to grill a split leg of lamb—and such a breeze to carve.*

> 1 5- to 6-pound leg of lamb
> 1 tablespoon lemon juice

75

1 clove garlic, split
1½ teaspoons salt
½ teaspoon ground cardamon
¼ teaspoon cinnamon
¼ teaspoon cloves
1 teaspoon ginger
1 teaspoon dry mustard
¼ teaspoon coarse black pepper
1 tablespoon chopped mint leaves
1 cup buttermilk
¼ cup melted butter or salad oil

Have butcher bone leg of lamb, cut it open and lay flat, butterfly-style. (Makes a flattish, boneless piece of meat about 2½ inches thick.) Rub all surfaces with lemon juice, garlic, and salt. Combine spices and rub well into lamb. Place in non-metallic dish. Add mint to buttermilk; pour over lamb. Marinate overnight, turning once or twice. Drain; save marinade. Place lamb, skin side up over medium-hot coals about 8 to 10 inches from heat. Broil and baste with butter and marinade, 45 minutes to 1 hour. Turn to brown fat side, after one-half hour. Do not overcook—keep slightly pink and juicy inside. Place on serving board, cut across grain into ½-inch thick slices. Good with a fresh tomato pilaf, spinach salad, and fruit. Makes 6 to 8 servings.

*Mabel Sherrill's Butterfly Lamb:* Easy and delicious! Replace marinade above with 1 packet Italian Dressing Mix for Salads prepared by packet directions. Substitute dry red wine for the liquid. Grill as above.


VEAL ANNETTE

*Buttered noodles or Parmesan-topped biscuits make a good accompaniment for this dish of veal simmered in a creamy, lemon sauce.*

1½ pounds thin veal round
    Salt, pepper, flour
2 tablespoons butter or margarine
2 two-inch strips lemon peel
1 10½-ounce can cream of chicken soup
¾ cup milk
½ cup cream

    1 cup pitted ripe olives
    1 8-ounce can small onions
    1 2-ounce can sliced mushrooms

Sprinkle veal on both sides with salt, pepper, flour. Pound into veal. Cut into 1-inch pieces. In heavy pan, brown slowly in butter. Add lemon peel, stir around to mix in lemon flavor. Add soup and milk. Blend, cover, and *simmer* until meat is tender, 30 minutes or more. Add cream, olives, drained onions, and mushrooms. Heat gently about 20 minutes longer. Serve from chafing dish or casserole warmer with hot, butter-tossed noodles or Parmesan-topped biscuits. Or you may transfer to casserole after browning and bake in moderate oven about 1 hour. Top with buttered crumbs after you add last ingredients. Makes 4 to 6 servings.

## SIX LITTLE ''BIRDS''

*Ageless and popular veal birds can be stuffed and browned ahead, then baked in the fragrant wine sauce to emerge from the oven when you choose to serve dinner.*

    1½ pounds thin veal round
        Salt, pepper, flour
     4 slices bacon, diced
     ⅓ cup chopped celery
     ⅓ cup chopped onion
     ¼ cup chopped parsley
     ½ cup chopped water chestnuts
     ½ teaspoon marjoram
      2 cups dry or toasted bread crumbs
  2 or 3 tablespoons salad oil
      1 cup chicken stock or consommé
     ½ cup red dinner wine

Cut veal into 6 or 8 pieces. Sprinkle with salt, pepper, and flour. Pound into both sides of meat. Fry bacon crisp; drain. In ¼ cup bacon drippings fry celery, onion, and parsley. Mix with water chestnuts, marjoram, bread crumbs, crumbled bacon. Moisten with about ¼ cup hot water or stock. Spread on veal, roll up tightly and fasten with string or

77

picks. Brown on all sides in hot oil. Put rolls in casserole. Add stock and wine to skillet. Bring to boil and stir up all the crumbs from bottom. Pour over veal rolls. Cover and bake at 350° 1½ hours. Thicken sauce with 1 tablespoon flour moistened in a little water if you like.

### FRITTA PICCATA

*We serve this with crisp zucchini slices and lots of extra lemon quarters to squeeze over the veal.*

> 1½ pounds veal round, sliced thin as for scallopini
> Salt and freshly ground pepper
> Flour
> 3 small zucchini
> 1 egg
> 1 cup fine white bread crumbs
> 6 tablespoons butter or margarine
> 4 tablespoons mild salad oil
> ¼ cup consommé
> Juice of ½ large lemon
> 1 tablespoon minced parsley
> 2 large lemons, quartered lengthwise

Cut veal into about 12 uniform scallops. Season with salt and pepper, and pound lightly. Dredge in flour; shake off excess. Wash zucchini. Cut each in 4 slices lengthwise. Dip in egg beaten slightly with a tablespoon water. Roll in crumbs to coat evenly. Let dry out a little. In large heavy skillet, heat about 2 tablespoons each butter and oil. Add veal and cook gently until golden brown on each side, about 5 minutes each. (If cooked too long or fast, veal will become tough and dried out.) Remove to warm platter; set in slow oven and cover loosely with foil to keep warm. Add 2 more tablespoons each of butter and oil to pan. Heat, and cook zucchini until light brown and crisp on each side. Arrange neatly on platter around veal. Add last 2 tablespoons butter to pan, pour in consommé and lemon juice. Let bubble up briskly and pour sizzling hot over the veal. Top with minced parsley. Garnish platter with 2 big juicy lemon quarters per person. Serve at once to 4.

# Feast on Beans, Pasta, Rice

These are savory, robust dishes—easy on your budget. Many of them have a rich heritage from the colorful cuisines of other lands. For instance, you'll find here interesting and easy-to-make variations of such classics as French cassoulet or Middle East pilaf along with a number of our own good American specialties.

Most of these recipes are full-meal dishes and especially suitable for pot luck and informal suppers, patio parties and the like.

### HOW TO COOK BEANS

In our opinion, nothing replaces overnight soaking—it seems to give a more tender bean and a richer flavor. This is the method we usually use. However, we also like the newer, quick-soaking method when we want cooked beans the same day.

These directions apply generally to all kinds of beans with some variation in cooking times. For example, garbanzos and black beans may require as much as 3 hours.

>     2 cups dried beans
>     6 cups water
>     2 teaspoons salt

Pick over beans, wash and cover with the 6 cups water. Soak overnight in cool place. Drain and cover with fresh water. Bring to boil and skim off foam. Turn heat low and simmer gently 1½ to 2 hours, or until tender. Add extra hot water as beans cook, if needed. Add salt last half hour. (Salting beans at the beginning tends to toughen them and retard cooking). Makes 5 to 6 cups cooked beans.

Seasoners such as salt pork, a ham bone, bacon or drippings, garlic, onions, or peppers may be cooked with beans, depending on the flavor you want in your finished dish.

*Quick-soak method:* Cover each cup of dried beans with 2½ cups water. Bring to boil and boil 2 minutes. Remove from heat. Cover tightly and allow to stand 1 hour. Cook as above.

### BLACK BEANS ALFRESCO

*The black beans, used so frequently in Brazilian and Cuban dishes, give this recipe its unusual flavor. Any dark bean may be used, such as red or pinto, but the flavor is not quite as distinctive.*

*The same is true of the fresh, sweet Italian sausages. Use our American pork sausage, if the other is not available, adding some typical Italian seasonings, such as oregano, sweet basil, and a few crushed fennel seeds. But do look for both the beans and sausages in Italian delicatessens or stores. Incidentally, there is a hot Italian sausage, too, but the sweet is better in this recipe.*

>     1 pound black beans
>     1 clove garlic, chopped
>     1 onion, chopped
>     ½ bay leaf, broken
>     ½ teaspoon mace

2 quarts water
2 teaspoons salt
1 cup dry red wine
1 pound fresh Italian sausage (sweet)
2 teaspoons butter or margarine
1 onion, sliced

Soak beans overnight in cool place in water 1 inch over top of beans. Rinse and put in large pot with garlic, onion, bay leaf, mace, and 2 quarts cold water. Bring to boil; lower heat and simmer gently 2½ to 3 hours. Season with salt last ½ hour. Add wine to bean pot; heat while frying sausage. Meanwhile cut sausages into 1-inch chunks. Put in skillet with the butter. Add onion when fat begins to fry out of sausage. Cook till soft and sausages are light brown. Scoop out half the chunks. Add one cup beans and liquid to skillet. Mash and stir over very low heat. Pour into bean pot. Transfer all to a large casserole, top with the sausage chunks. Bake in moderate oven 45 minutes to 1 hour, till chunks are browned and flavors well blended. Makes about 8 meal-size servings. Serve with a cool green salad, crisp bread, and a glass of red wine.

## HOT CHEESE BEANS

*An excellent barbecued meat accompaniment.*

1 cup dry limas
  Water
1 clove garlic
1 teaspoon salt
3 tablespoons butter
1½ cups grated sharp Cheddar cheese
¼ cup dry white wine
  Freshly ground black pepper

Soak limas overnight in 3 cups water. Add garlic; cover and boil gently until tender, about 1½ to 2 hours. Season with salt last ½ hour. Remove cover last few minutes to reduce some of liquid. Stir in butter, cheese, and wine. Cook uncovered over very low heat until cheese melts. Season with freshly ground pepper and additional salt if needed. Makes 4 servings.

81

BEAN RABBIT, MONTEREY

*Good Sunday night fare from a chafing dish or earthenware casserole kept hot over a table burner. It has an early-California air about it.*

> 2 cups cooked California pink, or red kidney beans
> 2 slices bacon, diced
> ½ cup chopped onion
> 1 cup diced fresh or canned tomatoes
> 2 cups (½ pound) diced Monterey Jack cheese or aged Cheddar
> ¼ cup diced canned pimiento
> 2 dried red chili peppers, deseeded
> ¼ cup dry white wine

Cook beans ahead of time by basic recipe. Fry bacon and drain. Put 1½ tablespoons bacon drippings in top of double boiler or in chafing dish. Add onion and tomato. Cover and cook until tender, about 10 minutes. Add cheese, pimiento, and crumbled peppers. Cook over hot water until cheese is melted, stirring all the time, 5 to 10 minutes. (Don't rush this part or the cheese will be tough and stringy.) Meanwhile heat together beans and wine. Blend into melted cheese mixture. Taste and add salt if needed. Serve hot with pumpernickel or dark rye bread. This must be kept *hot* or it will harden. However, any left over may be reheated slowly over hot water. Serves 4.

SOUR CREAM BEAN GOULASH

*A quick and easy meal in a dish.*

> ½ cup chopped onion
> ¼ cup chopped green pepper
> 1 chopped clove garlic
> ¼ cup salad oil
> 1 pound ground beef chuck
> 1 can condensed tomato soup
> ½ cup sour cream
> 3 cups cooked or canned drained kidney beans
> 1 tablespoon Worcestershire sauce
> 2 teaspoons paprika
> 1 teaspoon salt

Fry onion, pepper, and garlic in oil until soft. Add beef; cook and stir until meat loses red color. Stir in soup, sour cream, beans, Worcestershire sauce, paprika, and salt. Cover and heat gently until flavors blend, about 10 minutes. (Do not boil.) Makes 4 servings.

## GARBANZOS, NORTH BEACH

*These crisp round beans that traditionally accompany antipasto foods in San Francisco's Italian restaurants make a delightful salad for buffet or barbecue parties.*

> 2 cups cooked or canned garbanzo beans (chick-peas)
> 1 clove garlic, diced
> ¼ cup olive oil
> ¼ cup minced parsley
> 2 tablespoons diced pimiento or fresh sweet red pepper
> 2 tablespoons dry white table wine
> 1 teaspoon wine vinegar
>   Salt
>   Cracked or coarsely ground black pepper
>   Thin strips Italian salami

Drain garbanzos. Add diced garlic to olive oil and pour over beans. Sprinkle with rest of ingredients except salami. Mix well and season to taste with salt and pepper. Chill. At serving time top with strips of salami. Makes 3 to 4 servings.

## CASSOULET

*In France this delicious casserole is usually made with white beans, and several savory meat seasoners such as lamb, pork rinds, bacon, sausage, and preserved goose. This simplified version uses ground beef, fresh pork and garlic sausage with the traditional white wine and herb seasonings.*

> 1 pound white beans cooked by directions below (use small
>     whites, navy beans, limas)
> 3 tablespoons butter
> ½ pound fresh pork sausage
> 2 garlic sausages, sliced (smoked type, such as Polish, etc.)

83

1 onion, sliced
1 clove garlic, minced
1 pound ground beef chuck
1 teaspoon salt
   Freshly ground black pepper
1 cup dry white wine
1 cup tomato sauce
1 cup bean cooking liquid
½ teaspoon dried thyme
1 cup coarse dry bread crumbs
2 tablespoons chopped parsley

*Ahead of time, cook beans this way:* Soak 1 pound beans in 2 quarts water 4 or 5 hours. Add 1 whole onion stuck with 2 cloves, 1 bay leaf, a sprig of parsley, and ¼ pound salt pork, diced. Bring to boil, then simmer gently until tender, about 1½ hours. Season last half-hour with salt to taste, 1 to 1½ teaspoons. Add additional hot water if needed.

Heat 1 tablespoon butter till bubbly. Add fresh and garlic sausages. When the fat starts to cook out of them, add onion and garlic. Stir and fry till lightly browned. Push to side of pan. Crumble in beef. Cook only till it loses red color. Season with salt and pepper. In a large 3-quart casserole, put half the drained beans, top with half the meat mixture. Repeat layers. To frying pan add white wine, tomato sauce, 1 cup bean liquid, and thyme. Heat to simmering, pour over layers. Stir gently with fork so liquid runs all through. Bake in moderate oven (350°) 1 hour. Heat remaining 2 tablespoons butter till frothy. Stir in crumbs and parsley. Mix and spread over casserole. Bake 30 minutes. Makes about 8 servings.

HOW TO COOK AND DRESS SPAGHETTI
THE ITALIAN WAY

Spaghetti should literally *swim* in the water during cooking. For 1 pound spaghetti, bring 5 to 6 quarts water and 2 tablespoons salt to a rolling boil. (You may have to use two pots.) Add unbroken spaghetti all at once gradually pushing it down into the water as it softens. Keep water boiling all during cooking; stir occasionally. Cook until tender but not mushy. (Or "al dente" as the Italians say—still a little chewy and firm to the bite.) Regular spaghetti takes about 12 minutes, or follow package directions. Begin tasting a few minutes before you think it's done to get it just right.

Drain immediately; shake vigorously in collander. Do not rinse. Serve immediately—"dressing" it, like a salad, as the Italians do. In a big warm bowl put spaghetti and part of your sauce and cheese. Lift and toss gently with forks until spaghetti is coated. Serve with remaining sauce and cheese.

### PAISANO SPAGHETTI AND MEAT BALLS

*This combines the best features of many spaghetti recipes I've tried over the years.*

> Paisano Meat Balls
>       2 slices bread soaked in ⅓ cup water
>       ¼ cup minced onion
>       2 tablespoons minced parsley
>       1 egg, lightly beaten
>    1½ pounds ground beef*
>       1 teaspoon salt
>       2 tablespoons grated Parmesan cheese
>          Pinch each of nutmeg and cloves
>       ¼ cup olive oil

Soak bread in water while you prepare onion, parsley, and egg. Combine soaked bread (using all the liquid), meat, and the rest of ingredients except oil. Mix thoroughly with your hands until completely blended. Moisten hands and shape into 2 dozen small (1½-inch) meat balls— smaller than the usual Italian ones. Heat oil in heavy pan or skillet. Brown meat balls slowly on all sides, shaking pan frequently to keep balls round. Browning too fast makes them hard and crusty. Remove from pan. Use this same pan for sauce recipe, if you like.

*You may vary these meat balls, if you wish, by replacing ¼ pound beef with an equal amount of ground pork, pork sausage, fresh Italian sausage, or Prosciutto.

> Paisano Spaghetti Sauce
>       ¾ cup chopped onion

1 minced clove garlic
1 can Italian tomatoes (2 cups)
1 can tomato paste
1½ cups water
½ cup dry red wine or bouillon
1 teaspoon salt
1 teaspoon sweet basil
Tip of bay leaf
Pinch each of cloves and dried red pepper, if you like it spicy
Freshly ground black pepper
1 pound spaghetti
Grated Parmesan or Romano cheese

In meat ball pan, fry onion and garlic in the oil and drippings until soft. Stir in remaining sauce ingredients. Break up tomatoes against side of pan with fork. Simmer gently 30 minutes. Add meatballs to sauce; simmer very, very gently 20 to 30 minutes longer. (Please don't "boil" the meat balls!)

Cook spaghetti. Dress with sauce and cheese the Italian way as previously described. Serve with meat balls. This recipe makes 4 to 6 servings.

NOODLES ALLA ROMANA
*(Fettuccini al burro e parmigiano)*

*The absolutely perfect way to serve the fine noodles called fettuccini. Inspired by the dish Alfredo of Rome made famous—and about which so much has been written. Two things we have discovered: It requires fresh unsalted sweet butter and a bit of cream to round out the smoothness of the butter and Parmesan cheese blend. This then approaches the exquisite perfection of "Noodles Alfredo."*

8 ounces narrow egg noodles
Boiling salted water
½ cup sweet butter
6 tablespoons heavy cream
1 cup freshly grated Parmesan cheese

In large kettle of well-salted boiling water, add noodles gradually so boiling continues. Cook until barely tender, *al dente.* Meanwhile set butter on back of stove to soften. Add cream and Parmesan. Stir until it looks smooth and creamy. Keep warm but don't let it bubble. Drain hot noodles; plop into a warm shallow bowl. Pour creamy sauce over noodles. Toss and twirl with spoon and fork until thoroughly mixed. Serve pridefully to your happy guests. Makes 3 to 4 servings.

## HOMEMADE NOODLES

*Not at all difficult to make and worth every minute you spend on them. Your technique will improve with each batch you do. Toss in a hot dish with sweet butter and freshly grated Parmesan or Romano cheese as in Noodles Alla Romana.*

> 2½ cups all-purpose flour
> 2 large eggs
> 4 tablespoons cold water

Sift flour onto board. Make a well in center; drop in lightly beaten eggs. With your hands gradually work into flour with the water to make a stiff dough. Amount of water may vary a little. Knead and work the dough until it is elastic, about 10 minutes or so. It's fun, you'll discover. Divide into 3 pieces. Let rest about 10 minutes. Roll each into wafer-thin sheet at least 12 x 14. It may seem a little difficult at first—but stretch it gently over your palms. Let dry 15 to 20 minutes. Roll up from each end to center into double roll. With sharp knife cut into ¼-inch slices. Drop into large kettle of boiling salted water, letting noodles unroll as they fall. Boil 8 to 10 minutes. Drain into colander. *Do not rinse with cold water!* Shake colander vigorously. Put noodles in hot dish and toss with warm, soft sweet butter and Parmesan cheese.

## ELENA'S MACARONI SHELLS

*One of the most delicious ways to serve the attractive seashell-shaped pasta! The recipe originally came from one of my favorite persons, loving and beloved Elena Zelayeta—hostess, cook, and author of several books, including Elena's Fiesta Recipes.*

> 1 cup chopped onion
> 2 minced cloves garlic
> ¼ cup olive or salad oil
> 1 pound ground round steak

2 teaspoons salt
    Freshly ground black pepper
¼ teaspoon each dried rosemary, oregano, and sweet basil
2½ cups canned tomatoes
⅓ cup tomato paste
1 cup dry red wine
½ teaspoon sugar
1 12-ounce package large sea-shell macaroni
1½ cups shredded Parmesan cheese
¼ cup minced parsley

Stir and fry onion and garlic in hot oil until soft. Add beef, toss, and cook until it loses its red color. Season with salt, pepper, and crumbled herbs. Stir in tomatoes, tomato paste, wine, and sugar. Break up tomatoes against sides of pan with spoon. Simmer till flavors blend, 1 hour or more. Add additional hot water or wine if needed to keep sauce the thickness you like. Cook macaroni shells in a large kettle of boiling salted water by package directions. Drain, rinse in hot water. Drain again. Return to hot cooking pan or a warm serving dish. Add hot meat sauce, cheese, and parsley. Toss until macaroni is coated with a rich smooth blend of herb, sauce, and cheese. Serves 6 to 8.

POLENTA

In northern Italy polenta is a staple—here it is little known. This coarsely ground corn cereal with a rich sweet flavor is now available only in Italian stores. Perhaps, if there is more demand, more markets will carry it.

How to cook perfect polenta: Recipes usually call for 3 cups water to 1 cup polenta, but 4 cups water give it much better texture.

4 cups water
2 teaspoons salt
1 cup polenta meal
2 tablespoons butter or margarine
    Cheese to your taste

In top of double boiler over direct flame, heat 3 cups water and salt to boiling. Mix polenta with 1 cup cold water; slowly stir into boiling water. Add butter. Set over hot water; cover and cook 1 hour. Stir occasionally, preferably with a long handled wooden spoon (it sputters). The longer you cook it, the fluffier it looks, the richer is the good corn flavor.

It is delicious served with hamburger patties or steaks, chicken and gravy, or any meat or tomato sauce usually served with spaghetti. If you plan to make it into a highly seasoned casserole like the Shrimp Polenta, stir in some grated Cheddar or diced brick or Monterey Jack cheese at this point.

*Polenta made with finer, American-style corn meal* is not truly the same, but you can use it for all recipes which specify polenta. Use 3 cups water and 1 cup yellow corn meal. Season and cook as above but for only 30 minutes.

SHRIMP POLENTA
*Here is a good robust make-ahead dish for pot luck or outdoor parties.*

> 1½ pounds shrimp (fresh or frozen)
> 1 recipe cooked polenta
> ¾ cup grated sharp Cheddar cheese
> ½ cup grated Parmesan cheese
> 6 slices bacon, diced
> 1 onion, chopped
> ½ green sweet bell pepper, chopped
> 1 clove garlic, minced
> 1 no. 2½ can tomatoes (Italian tomatoes are best here)
> 1 teaspoon salt
> 1 teaspoon dried sweet basil

*Ahead of time, cook shrimp.* If raw shrimp are used, cook only until shells turn pink. Cool shrimp in cooking water; then shell and rinse out dark vein. If pre-shelled, cleaned frozen shrimp are used, drop into boiling salted water, then remove from heat immediately. Cool in liquid.

*Cook polenta.* Grate cheeses. Stir ¼ cup cheddar into cooked polenta. In a large heavy pan fry bacon crisp; drain. In the same pan, in 4 tablespoons of the drippings, fry onion, green pepper, and garlic lightly. Stir in tomatoes, salt. Crumble sweet basil in palms over the tomatoes.

89

Cover and simmer about 30 minutes. In large 2½- to 3-quart casserole, spread half the polenta. Next a layer of half the shrimp and bacon, then half the sauce. Shower with half remaining cheese. Repeat layers leaving a few whole shrimp to half-submerge in the top of the sauce for good looks. Bake in moderate oven (350°) 1 hour. Makes about 8 servings.

*To make ahead:* Prepare everything and assemble in the morning and refrigerate. Then put in oven while preheating it to 350°. Allow about 15 minutes extra cooking time.

### FLAKY RICE

*If you have a pet way of cooking rice, follow that. For years, though, this method has given me perfect rice, each grain separate, dry, and fluffy. It's cooked until tender but not mushy. If you like a moister rice, use a little more water and cook 5 minutes longer.*

Wash 1 cup raw, long-grain rice through several waters, rubbing it between your palms until water is clear. Then put into large heavy pan that has a *tight-fitting lid.* Add 1½ cups cold water and 1 teaspoon salt. Cover and bring to boil. Turn heat down at once to very lowest. Simmer 20 to 25 minutes without raising the lid or stirring. (Raising the lid allows the steam to escape; stirring makes the rice mushy and sticky.) To test for doneness, lift some rice lightly with a fork and taste. Cook a few minutes longer, if you like, but don't over-do it. Fluff up rice with fork. Remove from heat and let stand a few minutes before serving. Makes 2½ to 3 cups rice.

### QUICK RISOTTO WITH CLAMS

*A simplified version of an unforgettable dish we often enjoyed at the old Fior d'Italia restaurant in San Francisco. It always brings visions of the dapper little black-coated waiter and the big white ironstone platter piled high with tiny clams on a bed of fragrant pink risotto which he reverently served us. It needs only crusty bread and a light green salad.*

    1 onion, finely chopped
    ¼ cup olive oil
    1 cup raw rice, washed and drained

1 cup rich chicken stock
1 cup bottled clam juice
2 fresh tomatoes cut in wedges
2 tablespoons chopped parsley
¾ teaspoon salt
1 teaspoon dried sweet basil
Freshly ground pepper to taste
2 7-ounce cans minced clams

In heavy pan with tight fitting lid, fry onion in hot oil until soft and transparent. Add rice. Stir over medium heat until tanned in color but not brown. Add remaining ingredients including juice from the minced clams (but not the clams, for overcooking destroys their delicate flavor). Mix lightly. Put on lid and steam over very low heat until rice is tender and most of liquid absorbed, about 25 minutes. Stir in minced clams and a little more stock if needed. Cover and heat through enough to blend the flavors. Risotto should not be quite as dry as regular steamed or boiled rice. Makes 4 servings.

## STATION WAGON PILAF

*This one-pot dinner with its unusual combination of Near East foods and flavors is an ideal traveler since you can make it, carry it, keep it warm, and serve it in your electric skillet.*

1 pound lamb shoulder meat
¼ cup butter or margarine
1 cup raw rice
1 clove garlic, minced
1 onion, chopped
½ green bell pepper, chopped
1½ cups canned tomatoes
2 teaspoons salt
¼ teaspoon allspice
1 medium eggplant, cubed (2 to 3 cups)
½ cup grated Parmesan cheese

Cut lamb into small pieces, remove excess fat. In large heavy pan with tight-fitting lid, brown lightly in half the butter. Wash rice through several waters. Dry on paper towels. Add rest of butter to pan, toss in rice. Stir over medium heat till it starts to turn a soft wheat color. Add the garlic, onion, and pepper. Cook and stir till they are soft. Add tomatoes, salt, and allspice. Cover tightly and simmer gently about ½ hour. Stir lightly, then stir in egglant. Cover again and cook gently ½ hour more, or until the lamb is tender and most of the liquid absorbed. Avoid stirring too much—makes the rice mushy and sticky. Sprinkle with Parmesan cheese. Makes 4 to 6 servings.

# Vegetables with Eat Appeal

*If we borrowed a trick or two from the Orientals who have been quick-cook artists for centuries, we'd be sure to discover how good and appealing vegetables really are. Cooked the stir-fry way, they emerge brilliant and tenderly crisp—with the greens bright and shiny, the whites pearly and translucent, and the fresh natural flavor and vital values intact.*

Oriental Quick-Cook Vegetables

*The Oriental or stir-fry method is simplicity itself! But it does require preparation ahead and constant attention during the very few minutes of cooking. Needless to say, vegetables cooked this way must be served immediately. Especially suitable are green beans, asparagus, broccoli, cabbage, zucchini, carrots, green peppers, celery. (For do-ahead and serve-later vegetables, I include other recipes in this chapter.)*

Prepare the vegetables on a cutting board. This saves time, and wear and tear on your thumb. Wash, trim and arrange vegetables in rows.

With a sharp heavy French knife (or cleaver if you can handle it) slice through vegetables on an extreme slant. The thinner the slices, the faster they cook. You may also shred, dice, cube or cut in julienne strips, depending on recipe.

Heat a thin film of mild salad oil to near-smoking hot in a heavy pan— the traditional round bottomed Chinese wok, a chicken fryer or any heavy saucepan with tight lid. Add vegetables.

Stir and fry until colors deepen and vegetables glisten all over. Over a good hot fire, 4 average servings take about 2 minutes.

Add boiling stock or water, from 2 tablespoons to ½ cup. (The amount depends on vegetable, its freshness, how long you want to cook it, your pan and lid). Cover tightly and cook a few minutes longer, until vegetables are tender but still crisp. Reduce heat if you prefer a longer cooking time.

## American Quick-Sauté

*The examples of stir-fry cooking that follow are modifications of the above principles. Less oil is often suggested for the pre-sautéing, sometimes more water than the Orientals use and a fraction longer cooking time. These in consideration of our varied tastes and cooking pans. Don't skip the oil or butter sautéing entirely, however, since it's an important key in this method. It not only seals in flavors, juices, and food values—it gives that shine and "buttered taste" associated with good cooking. You'll be surprised how little extra butter or rich sauce you'll want with vegetables cooked this way.*

### SHINY CARROT SAUTÉ

Wash and scrape a bunch of fresh young carrots. Slice slant-wise for long ovals rather than the usual squatty rounds. Believe it or not, they taste different!

Heat 1 tablespoon oil in heavy pan. Add carrots. Keeping heat high, stir and fry about 2 minutes, until carrots are shiny and a deep rich color. Add ⅓ cup boiling water, about ½ teaspoon salt and ¼ teaspoon sugar. Cover tightly. When you hear the water sing again, turn heat low and simmer until tender but crisp, 7 to 10 minutes. Add a small dollop of butter, if you wish, but they truly don't need it. Serve at once.

94

### CELERY-CARROT SAUTÉ

Clean and slice 4 carrots as above. Strip any tough strings from 4 stalks of celery. The green Pascal variety is prettier, more flavorful. Slice thinly on a slant with a sharp heavy knife. Split wider, pale ends lengthwise. Mix with carrots. Cook same as above.

### CRISP BEANS WITH NUTMEG

Slice 1 pound fresh, trimmed green beans thin, on the slant or into julienne strips. Stir and fry in 2 tablespoons butter until deep green and shiny. Add ⅓ cup boiling chicken stock or water. Season with ¾ teaspoon salt. Cover and steam over low heat until crisp-tender, 5 to 10 minutes. Add freshly ground black pepper and grated nutmeg to taste—just a soupçon. (Instead of nutmeg a few snips of fresh dill or sweet basil also make good seasoners.)

### BEAN-BACON SAUTÉ

Select 1 pound slender, crisp-looking green beans; wash and trim. Slice on a slant into 1-inch pieces—thinner if you want to cook them more quickly. Slice 2 green onions and tops. Cook 3 strips diced bacon in saucepan until nearly done. To 2 tablespoons of the drippings, add onions and cook 1 minute. Add beans, stir and fry until bright green and shiny. Add ¾ cup boiling water. (Note: more water than is usual for sauté method because these beans are cooked longer.) Cover and simmer over low heat until tender, 20 to 30 minutes. Taste first, then add salt. Serve in small sauce dishes with all the good juice.

### CHINESE POD PEAS

*You needn't wait for a Chinese dinner to serve these succulent little peas-in-the-pod. They're wonderful anytime . . . especially with a delicately-seasoned chicken or veal dish. Many markets, at least in California, now carry them—often packaged in cellophane bags and kept in the refrigerator case where they stay sweet and fresh.*

For ½ pound, or a serving for two, wash and pull off end and strings. Heat 2 teaspoons corn or peanut oil in a heavy pan. Add peas; toss and stir over high heat until shiny and green color deepens. Add 2 to 4 table-

95

spoons boiling hot stock or water. Cover and steam 2 or 3 minutes at lower heat. You may need a little salt, but very little seasoning is needed for these gentle-flavored little delicacies.

### ZUCCHINI SAUTÉ

*Select small deep green zucchini or Italian squash, 4 to 6 inches long. Pale green patty pan summer squash or tender yellow crooknecks may be cooked the same way.*

Wash 6 to 8 small zucchini: cut off stems. Do not pare. Slice slant-wise into ovals. Slice 2 green onions and tops. Heat 1 tablespoon olive oil in saucepan; add onions and squash. Stir and fry 2 or 3 minutes, un-til shiny and bright green. Add ¼ cup boiling water, 1 teaspoon salt. Cover and steam crisp-tender at a lower heat, about 5 minutes. Add a few grindings of black pepper, and serve.

### BROCCOLI, CHINESE

*Here's a classic example of Chinese vegetable cookery! A little bit of meat combined with lots of crisp vegetable—to extend the flavors of both and make more servings.*

> ½ pound boneless fresh pork
> 2 tablespoons soya sauce
> 2 teaspoons sugar
> 1 tablespoon cornstarch
> 2 pounds fresh broccoli
> 3 tablespoons peanut or mild flavored oil
> ¾ cup hot water or chicken stock

Dice pork and add to a blend of the soya sauce, sugar and cornstarch. Marinate while preparing broccoli. Wash broccoli, strip off tough outer part of stalks. Split large stalks lengthwise into 1-inch stalks. Cut all on a slant into thin slices. Divide flowerets into small pieces. Heat oil in heavy pan or chicken fryer with lid. Toss in drained pork cubes. Stir and fry about 2 minutes. Add broccoli. Stir and fry until all pieces are shiny and a deep bright green in color. Add hot water or stock and re-maining marinade. Stir well. Cover tightly and simmer 3 to 4 minutes. Broccoli should still be bright green and crisp-tender. The sauce should be slightly thickened and delicious. Serve immediately. Makes 4 serv-ings.

## ITALIAN PEPPER SAUTÉ

*Cooking vegetables is a labor of love with the Italians, and the results are worth it.*

> 4 large, firm green peppers
> ¼ cup olive oil
> 1 minced clove garlic
> 1½ teaspoons salt
> Pepper
> Few snips fresh sweet basil, oregano or parsley, or a good pinch of dried

Wash peppers; remove stems and seeds. Cut lengthwise into strips about 1½ inches wide. Heat olive oil and garlic in large skillet or pan with lid. Add peppers, stir and toss until peppers are glistening with oil and tinged with brown in spots. (This takes about 5 minutes.) Sprinkle with salt and pepper to your liking. Cover tightly. Lower heat and simmer gently until crisp-tender, about 12 minutes. Add herbs and cook another 2 or 3 minutes. There's enough water in the peppers themselves if you keep the heat very, very low. Delicious with meats of all kinds. Makes 3 to 4 servings.

## MARIO'S BROCCOLI

*Cooked and sauced ahead, then baked later under a rich nut and cheese topping, this makes an excellent buffet vegetable.*

> 1 quart rich chicken stock
> 4 tablespoons flour
> Salt and freshly ground pepper
> Sage or poultry seasoning
> 1 tablespoon fresh lemon juice
> 2 tablespoons butter
> 2 pounds fresh broccoli
> ¾ cup dry bread crumbs
> 1 cup grated Parmesan cheese
> ½ cup sliced almonds or Brazil nuts
> Dots of butter

Blend a little stock with flour; smooth into rest of stock. Stir over medium heat until sauce thickens and flour is completely cooked. Season

97

to taste with salt, pepper, a dash of sage, lemon juice and 1 tablespoon butter. Cut broccoli into 4-inch lengths; split into quarters lengthwise. Slice end pieces. Place in pan containing 1 cup boiling salted water, heads on top. Cover and simmer until crisp-tender, 7 to 10 minutes. Raise lid occasionally to keep bright green color. Drain and place in buttered 2-quart baking dish. Cover with sauce. Mix crumbs with rest of butter and cheese. Spread on top. Sprinkle with nuts. Dot with butter. Bake at 350° about 45 minutes, or until bubbly hot and top is a toasted brown. Makes 6 servings.

## LETTUCE LEAF CORN

*Extra moisture in the form of wet lettuce and melted butter adds immeasurably to the sweet flavor of this foil-cooked corn. Remove husks and silk from corn. Wash and dip each ear in melted butter. Wrap in a wet lettuce leaf. Wrap securely in foil. Bake at 400° or on outdoor grill 30 to 40 minutes.*

## BAKED WHOLE EGGPLANT

*The world's easiest way to cook eggplant—a delicious vegetable usually so gussied up you seldom have a chance to taste its true flavor.*

Lay whole, unpeeled eggplant on the oven rack in a fairly hot oven, about 400°. Bake 1 hour for a medium-size eggplant, or until it feels soft and the skin looks lightly wrinkled. Split in half and fluff up with a fork as you do a baked potato. Season with salt, lots of freshly ground black pepper and a generous chunk of butter.

## STUFFED EGGPLANT SOUFFLÉ

*A light and fluffy filling is baked in eggplant half-shells.*

> 2 medium eggplants
> 1½ cups soft bread crumbs (about 4 slices bread)
> 2 tablespoons instant minced onion
> 2 tablespoons melted butter or margarine
> ½ cup chopped ripe olives or sautéed mushrooms
> 1¼ cups grated Cheddar cheese
> 4 eggs, separated

½ teaspoon crumbled oregano
¼ teaspoon allspice
    Salt and pepper
¼ cup grated Parmesan cheese

Simmer whole eggplants in 2 cups boiling, salted water about 15 minutes. Cut in half lengthwise and cut out center meat leaving a ¼-inch thick shell. Mash eggplant meat and combine with crumbs, onion, butter, ripe olives, cheese and egg yolks. Season with oregano, allspice, and salt and pepper to taste. Beat egg whites stiff; fold in lightly. Place eggplant shells in shallow pan with a little hot water in bottom. Fill with soufflé mixture. Sprinkle with Parmesan. Bake at 350° 45 minutes, or until puffed and light brown on top. Makes 4 luncheon-size servings.

ARTICHOKE DRESSINGS

*Artichokes, hot or cold, are delicious served with plain melted butter, mayonnaise, French dressing or Hollandaise, but I have a sentimental attachment for the Mayonnaise Diable, since that's how I first tasted them.*

*Mayonnaise Diable*
    ⅓ cup mayonnaise
    1 tablespoon Worcestershire sauce
    ½ teaspoon dry mustard

Blend all together and let stand several minutes before serving. Enough for 2.

SWISS TOMATOES

*Beautiful big tomatoes stuffed with Swiss cheese, cream and herb seasonings.*

4 large firm tomatoes
    Salt
2 cups grated, aged Swiss cheese
1 teaspoon instant minced or fresh grated onion
1 cup cream
2 tablespoons chopped parsley

⅓ cup chopped ripe olives
2 egg yolks, lightly beaten
¼ teaspoon each marjoram and thyme
   Dash of nutmeg
6 tablespoons fine bread crumbs
2 tablespoons melted butter or margarine

Halve tomatoes; scoop out insides leaving a thick shell. Salt lightly and up-end to drain. Mix rest of ingredients except crumbs and butter; add 1 teaspoon salt. Stuff into tomato shells and set in shallow baking dish. Top with crumbs and butter. Bake at 350° about 25 minutes. Serves 4 as luncheon dish, 8 as vegetable.

### TOMATOES AUX FINES HERBES

Cut 4 large firm tomatoes in halves. Fit snugly in a shallow stove-to-table baking dish. Sprinkle tops with salt and freshly ground black pepper. Mix 1 cup chopped fresh mushrooms and 1 cup fine, fresh bread crumbs. Toss for a minute or two in 3 tablespoons bubbling hot butter. Season with ½ teaspoon fines herbes. (Finely minced chives and parsley, with chervil, tarragon, or basil added if desired.) Heap onto tomatoes in firm mounds. Bake at 400° until tomatoes are slightly soft and crumbs are golden, 20 to 25 minutes. Serve from baking dish.

### GOLDEN CAULIFLOWER

*Cauliflower and cheese, broiled until puffy and bubbled with gold.*

1 head cauliflower
   Boiling salted water
½ cup grated, aged Swiss cheese
¼ cup mayonnaise
1 egg white
1 teaspoon lemon juice
2 tablespoons grated Parmesan cheese

Separate the cauliflower into flowerets, wash thoroughly. Drop into a sauce pan containing 1-inch of boiling salted water. Cook at a pretty fast clip until just tender, about 10 minutes. Drain and put in a shallow baking dish that can go under the broiler. Otherwise, protect the edge with a collar of foil. Combine the cheese and mayonnaise. Beat the egg white till stiff but not dry; fold in cheese. Add lemon juice and spread over the cauliflower. Sprinkle with grated Parmesan. Run under the broiler until sauce is puffed-up and golden looking, about 5 minutes. Keep the dish at least 6 inches from the broiler heat if possible. Makes 3 to 4 servings.

## SQUASH IN DILL CREAM

*Use little zucchini or scalloped patty pan summer squash for this delightful dish.*

Slice tender fresh squash into pencil-size sticks about 3 inches long. For 4 servings use 8 to 10 squash. In a saucepan with a tight lid, heat a tablespoon butter or salad oil, toss in squash and stir around until it's well coated and shiny. Add a little boiling water, ½ cup at the most, and 1 teaspoon salt. Cover tightly and simmer over very low heat until tender, 5 to 7 minutes. All the moisture should be just about evaporated; if not, leave uncovered a few minutes. Stir in ⅓ cup thick sour cream, ½ teaspoon dried dill weed or 1 tablespoon snipped fresh dill. Cover and heat through to blend the flavors.

*Zucchini vary throughout the country and are large in the East, where a "small" one might weigh ½ lb. By "small" I mean about 6 inches long.

## PERINO'S ZUCCHINI FLORENTINE

*Exactly as made and served at Perino's famous restaurant in Los Angeles. The tip Mr. Perino gave us about pre-frying the zucchini sticks ahead of time will enable you to have crisp, French-fried foods, even for a party. When you're ready to serve, it takes just a few seconds to brown them.*

Cut small, fresh zucchini into thin julienne strips. Dip in milk, then flour. Shake off excess flour, then dip in egg lightly beaten with a little milk. (About 2 tablespoons milk to each egg.) Drop into fine bread crumbs that have been sifted. Toss to coat evenly with crumbs. Let strips stand to dry out. Blanch or pre-cook by dropping into deep, hot fat (375°) and cook until pale gold in color. Drain on crumpled absorbent paper. At serving time, again drop into hot fat (375°). (Perino's restaurant uses a tasteless vegetable cooking oil.) Cook until crisp and golden brown. Sprinkle with salt and serve at once.

## EGGPLANT STICKS

*You can fry these by the directions for Perino's Zucchini Florentine or dip them in the batter given below:*

Peel eggplant and cut into thickish strips as you do for French fried potatoes. Dry on paper towels. Mix together for batter: 1¼ cups sifted flour, 1 teaspoon salt, 1 tablespoon salad oil, 2 lightly beaten eggs and 1 cup milk. Dip sticks in batter a few at a time. Fry in deep hot fat (365°) until light brown. Drain on paper towels.

## POTATOES ANNA

*Favored by gourmets for generations, this simple but elegant potato recipe can't be topped. Merely slice potatoes paper thin and bake in layers with butter. Turn out upside down in a crusty mound of golden perfection.*

Peel medium-small potatoes allowing one for each person and one or two extra "for the pot." Slice into rounds almost paper-thin. Drop into cold salted water; soak at least one-half hour. Dry on paper towels. Butter generously a round bottomed mold or pan. (Round bottomed glass casserole is ideal). Place layer of slightly overlapping slices in bottom and up sides. Season with salt and pepper; spread with about one table-spoon soft butter. Repeat layers, reversing direction of slices for each layer. Season and butter each (most classic recipes say ½ cup butter for six cups potato slices). Cover and bake at 425° 30 minutes. Uncover and bake 15 to 20 minutes longer, until potatoes are tender and bottom is browned. Invert over a serving dish brown side up.

*Chive accent:* The above is the classic version. At our house we sprinkle each layer with a few snipped fresh or frozen chives, using about 2 table-spoons in all.

# Bread Baking Revival

Hard to match is the nostalgic appeal of fragrant homebaked yeast bread. Perhaps that's why more and more women are learning to make a few special breads for their families and friends. I won't attempt to go into all the psychological aspects of it, but this bread-baking revival does seem to be a rebellion against so much "easy" living and a reversion to things of basic value. A number of my friends find time to bake a few loaves of bread and a couple of pans of rolls once a week.

I'm not suggesting that you go into competition with the good baker, only that you try baking occasionally, if for no other reason than to satisfy that "creative" urge. It's quite gratifying, and surprisingly enough, easier than you think once you get your hands into it. If you're timid about yeast dough, get the feel of it and discover how much fun it is with some of the recipes that start with a hot-roll mix. I include a sec-

*tion later. Soon you'll have enough confidence to tackle something made from scratch. Little suppers of homemade soup and homemade bread can make you famous.*

## CAPPY'S GOOD WHITE BREAD

*A perfect loaf of homemade bread! Not much kneading but two risings account for its fine light texture. Friends who are experienced bread bakers always comment on its wonderful quality and wheaty flavor.*

> 2 cakes compressed yeast
>    or 2 packages active-dry yeast
> ½ cup warm water
> 1 cup milk
> 1 tablespoon sugar
> 2 tablespoons butter or shortening
> 2 teaspoons salt
> 1 cup cold water
> 6 cups sifted all-purpose flour

Crumble or sprinkle yeast into the ½ cup warm (not hot) water. Stir to dissolve. Scald milk until bubbles appear around edges; add sugar, shortening, and salt. When shortening is melted, pour into large mixing bowl. Add the 1 cup cold water. When mixture is luke warm, stir in yeast. Mix in flour, using your hands towards the last. The amount of flour to make a medium-stiff dough may vary a little.

Place in large greased bowl. Cover with towel and let rise in warm place until doubled in bulk, about 1 hour. Punch dough down with your fist. Knead lightly on a floured board 2 or 3 minutes. Put into greased bowl; cover and let rise again in warm place until doubled, 45 to 60 minutes (second rising usually takes less time).

Punch dough down again and cut in half. Knead each part a few minutes until smooth and springy. Shape into loaves and put in greased metal loaf pans. Cover and let rise in warm place until nearly double in size, about 1 hour. Bake at 375° 50 to 60 minutes. While warm brush crust with butter. Remove bread from pans and cool on wire racks. Makes 2 loaves.

BUTTERMILK RYE BREAD

*A moist, fine-textured loaf with the deep rye flavor and crustiness of Old World bread. Make it the day before so it will slice easily.*

    2 cups buttermilk
    2 cakes compressed yeast
    2 tablespoons brown sugar or molasses
    2 tablespoons salad oil
    2 tablespoons caraway seeds
    3 cups sifted all-purpose flour
    2 teaspoons salt
    3 cups unsifted rye flour

Heat buttermilk to lukewarm. (Separation caused by heating does not affect flavor.) Put in large warm bowl; crumble in yeast. Stir until well mixed. Add brown sugar, salad oil, and caraway seeds. Set aside ½ cup all-purpose flour for kneading. Resift rest with salt; mix with rye flour. Add half the flour to yeast, beating it in hard. Place bowl in warm place, cover with towel, and let rise until double in bulk, 1 to 1½ hours. (Rye bread takes longer than white.) With your hands or a big spoon work rest of mixed flour into dough—get your hands right into it.

Turn this rough-looking dough out onto board lightly sprinkled with part of your extra flour. Knead until smooth and springy, using extra flour sparingly. Place in greased bowl. Set in warm place again. Cover and let rise until double in size, 60 to 75 minutes.

Punch dough down, turn onto board and cut in half. Flatten and shape as follows: Mold into 2 long pointed cylinders and place on greased baking sheets. (This makes the traditional, crusty, Old-World loaf.) Or mold to fit into 2 greased metal loaf pans—makes a softer loaf with less crust. Cover and let rise in warm place until nearly doubled in size, 45 minutes to 1 hour. With sharp knife, cut 3 diagonal slashes, across top of long rolls. Bake at 375° 50 to 60 minutes. Crust should be brown and bread sound hollow when tapped on top. Remove to wire racks to cool.

*For a hard glazed crust:* Brush hot loaves with egg white and sprinkle with caraway seeds. For a soft crust, brush with butter while hot.

*A stunt I practice with this spectacular loaf: Time it to be just about ready to remove from the oven when dinner guests arrive. The heavenly fresh yeast bread aroma is devastating.*

> 2 cups milk
> 2 tablespoons sugar
> 1½ teaspoons salt
> 2 cakes compressed yeast
> 6 tablespoons shortening and butter (half and half)
> 4 eggs
> 5¼ cups sifted all-purpose flour

Heat milk till bubbles form around edges. In very large bowl, pour milk over sugar and salt. Stir till milk is luke warm. Crumble in yeast. Stir till mixed and dissolved. With wooden spoon stir in melted shortening and butter. Beat in eggs, and almost 5 cups flour in small portions. Beat until smooth, about 100 strokes. Cover with greased paper, then tea towel. Let rise until very light and spongy looking, about 1 hour. (You may place in refrigerator and beat dough down with wooden spoon to slow the rising if you want the bread to come out of the oven at a little later hour.) Turn light dough out onto cloth or board floured with remaining ½ cup flour. Knead lightly by lifting corners of cloth and folding dough over a few times. Place in greased 10-inch tube pan or angel food cake pan. Let rise to 1 inch from top of pan, about 45 minutes. Bake at 350° 50 minutes to 1 hour, until very crusty and golden brown on top, completely done inside. Turn out on big serving plate. Cut in thick wedges with serrated bread knife (use a sawing motion so as not to crush the tender fresh bread). Serve hot with plenty of butter. Toast next day or wrap and freeze for later use.

HERB BATTER BREAD

*This open textured round loaf looks like a giant popover and is made from batter rather than a kneaded yeast dough. An easy bread for the beginner with yeasts.*

> 1¼ cups milk
> 1 teaspoon caraway seeds

  1 teaspoon poppy seeds
  1 teaspoon instant minced onion
  1 teaspoon dried chervil
 ½ teaspoon dried marjoram
  2 tablespoons sugar
  2 teaspoons salt
  4 tablespoons butter or margarine
  2 packages or cakes yeast
 ½ cup warm (not hot) water
  2 eggs, beaten
 ½ teaspoon grated nutmeg
 4½ cups sifted all-purpose flour
   Poppy seeds, coarse salt, and minced onion for top

Heat milk with seeds, minced onion, herbs, sugar, and salt to scalding. Stir in butter until melted. Cool to lukewarm. Sprinkle or crumble yeast into water; stir until dissolved. Stir in milk mixture, eggs, nutmeg, and flour. Beat vigorously about 2 minutes. Cover and let rise in warm spot until more than doubled in bulk. The batter looks somewhat rough and moist with small bubbles just under the surface—not tightly stretched as in regular yeast dough. Stir batter down with your fist or a wooden spoon. Beat hard ½ minute or more. Turn into a greased 2-quart casserole or a small 8-inch tube pan. If you want to give this a very professional look, sprinkle top with extra poppy seeds, coarse salt, and a teaspoon instant minced onion rehydrated in a little water. Let rise 20 minutes now if you wish or put in oven at once. Bake at 375° 45 minutes to 1 hour. Turn out of pan onto wire rack; cool. Serve warm in thick slices with sweet butter. This light, open textured bread slices more easily if baked ahead and cooled. Just before serving slice with a serrated knife, reassemble, and heat in foil a few minutes.

FEAST BREAD

*Flavored with anise seeds, this crusty round loaf will remind you of the fragrant Italian holiday breads.*

  1 cup milk
  1 cake compressed yeast*
 3½ to 4 cups sifted all-purpose flour

⅓ cup shortening
½ cup sugar
1 egg
1½ teaspoons salt
¼ teaspoon nutmeg
2 tablespoons crushed anise seeds or ¾ teaspoon anise extract
½ cup seedless raisins

Scald milk and cool to lukewarm. Crumble in yeast; stir until dissolved. Blend in 1½ cups flour. Cover with towel and let stand in warm place until very light, about 1½ hours. Cream shortening and sugar together thoroughly. Beat in egg, salt, nutmeg and anise. Stir into yeast sponge. Blend in half the remaining flour. Rinse raisins; dry on paper towels and stir into dough. Add remaining flour to make a soft dough. Cover and let rise until doubled in volume, about 1½ hours. Punch down and shape into round loaf. Place on greased cooky sheet or in round cake pan. Grease top. Let rise until doubled in volume, about 1 hour. Bake in a 350° oven 45 to 50 minutes. Cool on wire rack.

*For active dry yeast: Use ¾ cup milk. Sprinkle package active dry yeast onto ¼ cup warm water. Stir till dissolved; let stand. Stir into lukewarm milk.

### MARVA'S BUTTER ROLLS

*One rising only—just in the pans—yet these are feather-light and have a thin, flaky crust somewhat like Danish pastry or French croissants.*

1 cake compressed yeast
1½ cups lukewarm water
1 egg
2 tablespoons sugar
3½ cups sifted all-purpose flour
1 teaspoon salt
Flour for kneading
½ cup soft butter or margarine (or ¼ cup of each)

Crumble yeast into lukewarm water. Stir until dissolved. Add egg and sugar. Beat vigorously. Sift flour and salt. Stir into yeast in small portions beating very hard after each addition. The amount of flour varies from 3½ to 4 cups, but dough should be barely stiff enough to handle. Turn dough onto floured board or cloth. Knead until smooth and elastic, about 5 minutes. (Approximately ½ cup more flour will be used.) Roll dough into a 15-inch circle. Spread with ¼ the soft butter. Fold in half, then fold again. Roll into circle again, spread with butter. Spread and fold 4 times total. Roll out ½ inch thick. Cut into rounds to fit in muffin pans. Put in pans; let rise 1½ to 2 hours. Bake at 400° 10 to 15 minutes, or until brown—and delicious. Makes about 2 dozen 2½-inch rolls.

MILL VALLEY SWEET ROLLS

*I usually make a dozen cinnamon nut rolls, then use the remaining dough for mixtures of my own invention: Lime marmalade and coconut or grape jelly and cream cheese. You can dream up some of your own!*

    ½ cup milk
    2 teaspoons sugar
    ½ cup cold water
    1 cake compressed yeast
    3½ cups sifted all-purpose flour
    ¼ cup sugar
    1 teaspoon salt
    3 tablespoons melted butter or salad oil
    2 eggs, beaten
      Filling (recipes below)
      Powdered sugar icing

Heat milk until bubbles form around edges. Stir in 2 teaspoons sugar and cold water. When lukewarm crumble in yeast; stir until dissolved. Stir in about 1 cup of the flour; blend smooth. Cover with towel; and let rise in warm place until doubled in bulk, about 1 hour. Stir in remaining ingredients and rest of flour. Mix smooth. Cover and let rise in warm place until doubled, about 1 hour.

Turn onto floured board and knead dough a few seconds, until smooth and easy to handle. Divide in half. Roll each into oblong about 8 x 12 inches. Spread with filling; roll up tightly from long side as in jelly roll.

Pinch edges together to seal. Cut into 1-inch slices. Place in greased baking pan, about 9 x 11 inches. Cover and let rise until double in size, 30 to 45 minutes. Bake at 350° 30 minutes. Ice while warm if desired. Makes 2 dozen rolls. Can be doubled.

Besides the favorite cinnamon and nut filling the possibilities for variety seem limitless with this satiny yeast dough. These recipes make enough to spread 1 dozen rolls only.

*Ginger-coconut filling:* Spread rolled dough with 2 tablespoons soft butter, ¼ cup ginger marmalade, ½ cup flaked coconut.

*Grape-cream cheese filling:* Spread rolled dough with 1 tablespoon soft butter blended with one 3-ounce package soft cream cheese, 6 tablespoons grape jelly or marmalade.

*Lime dream filling:* Spread rolled dough with 2 tablespoons soft butter, ¼ cup lime marmalade, ¼ cup each flaked coconut and chopped toasted almonds. Put 1 teaspoon grated fresh lime rind in powdered sugar icing (below) and use 2 teaspoons Kahlua liqueur for part of the cream if you like.

*Powdered sugar icing:* For 2 dozen rolls, blend into 1 cup sifted powdered sugar about 2 tablespoons cream or evaporated milk. It should have texture of heavy cream. Too thick makes a heavy, "coated" roll— too thin runs down into rolls too much. Flavor with ½ teaspoon vanilla extract. We also like the zest of a little grated orange rind.

ORANGE TEA BREAD

*Raisins and a whole orange ground together account for the wonderful fruit flavor of this quick bread. It slices more easily and tastes better when made the day before.*

> ⅔ cup dark seedless raisins
> 1 large orange
> 2½ cups sifted all-purpose flour
> 1 teaspoon salt
> ½ teaspoon soda
> 1½ teaspoons baking powder
> 2 eggs
> ⅔ cup sugar

1 cup water
⅓ cup melted butter or margarine
1 cup chopped walnuts

Rinse and dry raisins. Quarter unpeeled orange and remove seeds. Put raisins and orange through food chopper using medium blade, being careful to catch all the orange juice. Sift flour with salt, soda, and baking powder. Beat eggs just enough to mix well; stir in sugar, water, butter, raisin-orange mixture, and all the juice. Add flour mixture and nuts all at once. Stir just enough to blend, but do not beat. Turn into greased and floured metal loaf pan (8½ x 4½ x 3 inches). Bake at 350° about 1 hour. Remove from pan; cool on wire rack.

DANISH CROWN CAKE

*Elegant and rich, almost like cake—but not as sweet. We serve it at holiday time with eggnog.*

Soft butter for pan
½ cup thinly sliced almonds
2 tablespoons sugar
1 teaspoon cinnamon
1 cup sifted all-purpose flour
½ teaspoon baking powder
¼ teaspoon soda
Dash of salt
½ cup butter or margarine
½ cup sugar
2 eggs
6 tablespoons sour cream
Powdered sugar

Butter generously an 8-inch ring mold and coat all over with about half the almonds. Mix rest with 2 tablespoons sugar and cinnamon. Sift together flour, baking powder, soda and salt. Cream the ½ cup butter and ½ cup sugar together thoroughly. Beat in eggs, one at a time. Alternately blend in dry mixture and sour cream. Spread half the batter in mold, top with half the almond-sugar mix. Repeat with rest of batter and almonds. Bake at 350° about 30 minutes, or until golden brown.

111

Turn out on rack, sprinkle with powdered sugar. Makes 6 to 8 servings. Serve warm or cold.

## BRAN MUFFINS

*Moist, yet light . . . the best I've ever tried.*

>     ¼ cup shortening
>      1 tablespoon butter
>     ¾ cup dark raisins
>      2 eggs
>      2 tablespoons sugar
>      2 tablespoons molasses
>    1½ cups buttermilk
>      2 cups all-bran cereal
>      1 cup sifted all-purpose flour
>      1 teaspoon soda
>      2 teaspoons baking powder
>     ½ teaspoon salt

Melt shortening and butter together; cool slightly. Rinse and drain raisins. Beat eggs and stir in sugar, molasses, buttermilk, bran, and raisins. Let stand 5 minutes. Sift flour with soda, baking powder, and salt. Stir lightly into bran mixture along with shortening. Fill greased muffin tins ⅔ full. Bake at 400° about 25 minutes. Let stand 5 minutes. Remove from pans. Serve hot with butter, and more butter. Makes 16 large muffins or 2 dozen tiny ones.

## ADENE'S GREEN CHILE BREAD

*A very unusual hot bread. Try it in place of potatoes or corn with grilled chicken, hamburger steaks, hearty bean casseroles. From Adene Wilson, former food editor of the* Los Angeles Examiner.

>      1 4-ounce can green chiles
>      1 cup grated sharp Cheddar cheese
>      1 cup corn meal
>    1¼ teaspoons salt
>    2½ teaspoons baking powder
>     ¼ teaspoon soda

2 eggs
1 cup cream-style corn
½ cup plus 2 tablespoons buttermilk
⅓ cup fresh bacon drippings

Rinse chiles, remove seeds, and spread flat to dry on paper towels. Grate cheese. Mix cornmeal, salt, baking powder, and soda. Beat eggs lightly. Stir in corn, buttermilk, dry mixture, and drippings. Mix only enough to blend. Spread half the batter in greased 8-inch square pan. Cover with chiles, cut in 1-inch strips, half the cheese. Spread with rest of batter, then cheese. Bake at 350° 45 minutes to 1 hour. Cut in squares and serve warm as bread or to replace potatoes or rice.

*Pimiento bread:* For a milder flavor, or if you can't find the canned green chiles in your stores, use 1 4-ounce can whole pimientos in place of them. Drain and cut in 1-inch strips as above.

## LEMON SCONES

*There is an excellent scone mix on the market—and I keep it on my shelf all the time—but, you'll never be a great cook, or even just good if you depend on mixes for everything. The lemon sugar topping on these makes them sparkle and smell very tempting.*

2 cups sifted all-purpose flour
3 teaspoons baking powder
1 teaspoon salt
3 tablespoons sugar
6 tablespoons butter or margarine
⅓ cup dried currants
1 egg
   Cream (about ½ cup)
2 tablespoons grated lemon rind

Sift together flour, baking powder, salt and 1 tablespoon sugar. With pastry blender, cut in butter until mixture is crumbly. Add currants. Beat egg lightly with fork; add enough cream to make ¾ cup. Stir into dry mixture to form a soft dough. On floured board, fold dough over itself 4 or 5 times; divide in half. Pat each half into an 8-inch circle, slightly flattened at edges, thicker in the middle. Cut into 6 wedges. Brush each with cream. Mix lemon rind and rest of sugar. Sprinkle evenly over scones. Place on cooky sheet and bake at 450° 12 to 15 minutes. Serve hot with butter. Makes 12 scones.

## START WITH A MIX

*Mixes certainly have a place in our contemporary kitchens and many of them have earned our warm regard and respect. They're fun to use and give dependable results. To my way of thinking, however, they shouldn't be considered as the end and all of your cooking, but merely the means to faster meals. They make effective quick-starters for some spectacular homemade creations. The word "creations" is used advisedly, for you can be imaginative with mixes and other convenience foods by adding fresh spices and seasonings, herbs and seeds, fruits, nuts, unusual toppings, and such. You'll get the idea from the recipes in this section.*

### BLUE CHEESE STRIPS
*Flaky with blue cheese and butter, these are fine baked ahead and reheated.*

Make dough from hot-roll mix; let rise in warm place till doubled in bulk. Knead lightly on floured board and roll very thin into oblong. Spread a blended mixture of ⅓ cup soft butter and ⅓ cup blue cheese over one half the dough. Fold over and seal edges. Roll again into rectangle. Fold in thirds, the ends toward the center. Roll once more into rectangle. Cut into strips about 1 x 4 inches. Place on greased pan. Brush with beaten egg white, and sprinkle with poppy seeds if you like. Cover with a towel; let rise until doubled. Bake at 425° 8 minutes. Serve hot or reheat at 400° a few minutes. Also good served cold like bread sticks.

### CHEDDAR ROLLS
*The perfect partner for one of the hearty bean dishes.*

> 1 package hot-roll mix
> ⅓ cup chopped green onion or 1 tablespoon instant minced onion

114

2 tablespoons water
¼ cup soft butter or margarine
2 cups grated sharp Cheddar cheese
¼ cup chopped parsley
1 can (⅔ cup) chopped ripe olives
1 teaspoon crumbled oregano

Make up hot-roll mix by package directions. Let rise till doubled; punch down and knead lightly on floured board. Saute onion in a little of the butter or soak minced onion in a little hot water. Cream soft butter with cheese, mix in onion and rest of ingredients. Divide dough in half. Roll each into oblong about 8 x 14 inches. Spread with cheese and roll up like jelly roll. Cut into 1½-inch slices. Put cut side down in greased muffin pans. Let rise 30 to 45 minutes, until double in size. Bake at 400° 10 to 14 minutes. Makes 18 to 24 rolls.

## HOT TEAR-OFF LOAF

*Made to match an interesting loaf I saw in a bakery window one night. Simply buttered slices of yeast dough, stacked on edge in a loaf pan and baked.*

1 package hot-roll mix or a good yeast-roll recipe
⅓ cup soft butter or margarine
2 tablespoons toasted sesame seeds

Prepare hot-roll mix by directions on package. Cover; let rise till doubled in bulk. Punch down with fist and knead lightly on floured board or cloth. Roll into square (12 x 12 inches). Spread thickly with soft butter; sprinkle with toasted sesame seeds. Cut into three long strips 4 inches wide. Cut each strip into oblongs 4 x 2 inches. Stack several pieces together evenly, butter side up. Put stacks on edge, the 4-inch side down in greased large glass loaf pan (10 x 5 x 3 inches). Continue until pan is full and loaf looks like an accordion. Let rise till doubled in size, almost to the top of the pan, 45 minutes to 1 hour. Bake at 375° 25 to 30 minutes. Serve hot in napkin-lined basket, tearing off the hot buttery slices as you eat them. Wrap in foil to reheat . . . it's almost as delicious. For smaller loaf pan (9 x 5 x 3 inches) use ⅔ of dough. Make rest into fan-tan rolls by same method and bake in muffin tins.

*Parmesan loaf:* Cut rolled dough with round biscuit cutter. Dip in melted butter and ⅔ cup grated Parmesan cheese. Stand on edge in loaf pan (9 x 5 x 3 inches), overlapping each two slightly in center. Sprinkle with any left-over cheese. Let rise and bake as above.

*Freezer note:* This freezes well. Cool and wrap in foil. Reheat unthawed in foil at about 400° for 15 minutes.

## SALTY CHEESE CRESCENTS

*The salty tang of anchovy paste in the cream cheese filling makes these rolls especially complimentary to salads.*

> 1 package hot-roll mix or your favorite yeast roll dough
> ¼ cup soft butter or margarine
> 1 3-ounce package cream cheese
> 1 tablespoon anchovy paste

Prepare hot-roll mix, cover and let rise as directed on package. Punch down with fist and knead lightly on floured board or cloth. Divide into 2 balls for easier handling. Roll each into thin circle hardly ¼ inch thick. Cream together butter, cream cheese, and anchovy paste. Spread over dough. Cut into 8 or 10 pie-shaped wedges. Beginning at outside edge of each wedge roll up towards point. Place with point down on greased pan. Curve ends slightly to form crescent. Cover and let rise until doubled in size, about 30 minutes. Bake at 400° 12 to 15 minutes. Serve hot or reheat. Makes 18 to 20 crescents.

## BUTTER NUT WHIRLS

*An almond and sweet butter filling makes these coffee cakes rich and festive for holiday feasting.*

> 1 package hot-roll mix or ½ recipe Mill Valley Sweet Rolls
> 1 egg, unbeaten
> 6 tablespoons sugar
> ½ cup sweet butter
> 1 cup brown sugar, packed
> 1 teaspoon nutmeg
> 1 cup finely-chopped, lightly toasted almonds or pecans

½ teaspoon cinnamon
Almond halves

Prepare hot-roll mix using ¾ cup water, the egg and 2 tablespoons of the sugar. Cover and let rise till doubled in bulk. Using your fingertips, blend soft butter, brown sugar, nutmeg, and chopped nuts. Divide dough for easier handling and roll thin into 2 long narrow oblongs. Spread with filling to within 1 inch of edge. Roll up tightly from long side and seal in filling by pinching edges of dough together. Gently stretch and elongate rolls. Coil each into greased 8-inch round cake pan leaving space between coils. Flatten slightly. Cover and let rise until doubled, 30 to 40 minutes. Mix cinnamon with remaining sugar and a handful almond halves. Sprinkle over tops. Bake at 375° for 30 to 35 minutes. Serve warm. Makes 2 whirls.

### QUICK SALT STICKS

*Yeast bread flavor that starts with biscuit mix. If you prefer them very crisp and crunchy, like the bakery kind, bake at least 15 minutes—then leave in the oven about 5 minutes after the heat is turned off.*

⅔ cup milk
1 cake compressed yeast
2 cups biscuit mix
2 tablespoons oil or melted shortening
Egg yolk
Coarse salt
Caraway seeds or poppy seeds

Heat milk to lukewarm. Crumble in yeast. Stir into biscuit mix with shortening. Knead on board lightly sprinkled with biscuit mix, until smooth, about ½ minute. Pinch off into 16 to 20 balls. With palms roll each ball into cylinder. Then flatten with rolling pin into ribbon about 8 inches long. Brush with egg yolk beaten with a tablespoon water. Sprinkle with salt and seeds. Hold strip at both ends. Twist in opposite directions. Brush again with yolk and sprinkle with seeds. Lay on greased cooky sheet, pressing ends down to keep from unrolling. Let rise until light, 20 to 30 minutes. Bake at 425° 10 to 12 minutes.

*Parker House biscuits:* Roll dough about ⅓ inch thick. Cut with small biscuit cutter and brush with melted butter. Fold over like Parker House rolls. Brush with butter. Let rise on greased cooky sheet until doubled. Bake at 400° 15 to 20 minutes.

*Parmesan tops:* Roll dough and cut with small cutter. Brush with melted butter; then dip in grated Parmesan cheese. Let rise until light, or doubled, depending on size. Bake at 425° 10 to 12 minutes. Wonderful with salads.

### ONION STICKS

*These go to luncheon with a salad or bowl of good soup. They usually disappear by the basketful at our outdoor parties.*

> ¼ cup butter or margarine
> 1 tablespoon instant minced onion
> ⅔ cup grated sharp Cheddar cheese
> 1 teaspoon celery seed
>    Generous dash seasoned salt
> 2 cups biscuit mix
> ⅔ cup milk

Melt butter in shallow pan (13 x 9 inches). Cover evenly with 2 teaspoons minced onion. Stir remaining onion, cheese, celery seed, and seasoned salt into biscuit mix. Add milk; mix to soft dough. Knead lightly on floured board. Roll into oblong 6 x 10 inches. Cut in half lengthwise, then into strips about 1 x 3 inches. Turn in onion-butter mixture to coat evenly. Bake at 425° about 15 minutes, until sticks are golden and onion is crisp and toasted. Makes 20 sticks.

### PLEATED SESAME LOAF

*Butter-crusted biscuits, lavishly topped with cheese and toasted sesame seeds. A delicious quick hot bread for fruit salads, molds, and the like.*

> ⅓ cup butter or margarine
> 3 cups biscuit mix (your own or packaged)
> 1 cup milk
> ½ cup grated Parmesan cheese

2 tablespoons toasted sesame seeds and/or 2 tablespoons each of snipped chives, parsley, and caraway seeds

Melt butter, put in shallow bowl. Combine biscuit mix and milk, stir to a smooth dough. Knead lightly on floured board and roll into oblong about ⅓ inch thick. Cut into 18 round biscuits with 2½-inch cutter. Dip each biscuit in melted butter, then in Parmesan cheese. Stand two biscuits at a time on edge in glass loaf pan (9 x 5 x 3) overlapping them slightly where they meet in the center. Sprinkle with a few sesame seeds as you fill the pan till it looks like an accordion pleated affair. Sprinkle rest of seeds on top. Bake at 425° about 20 minutes, until golden brown and puffed up. Serve hot in a napkin-lined basket.

*To vary the seasonings:* Use any one or several of the suggested herbs and seeds with the butter and Parmesan.

PARMESAN PUFFS

2 cups biscuit mix
⅔ cup milk
⅓ cup melted butter or margarine
⅔ cup grated Parmesan cheese

Combine mix and milk to soft dough. Roll into rectangle 10 x 12 inches. Cut into strips 1 x 5 inches. Dip in butter then in cheese. Holding ends, twist in opposite directions; place on cooky sheet. Press ends down firmly to hold twist. Bake at 450° 10 to 15 minutes. Makes 2 dozen.

FROSTED BLUEBERRY CAKE

*Rich, moist coffee cake made from biscuit mix.*
Combine 2 cups biscuit or scone mix, 1 teaspoon cinnamon, 1 egg, 2 tablespoons melted shortening, ¾ cup sour cream. Stir only until dry ingredients are dampened. Fold in ¾ cup fresh or frozen blueberries (or drained canned), ½ cup chopped walnuts. Spread in greased 8-inch, round, 1½-inch deep pan. Bake at 400° about 30 minutes. Blend ½ cup powdered sugar into 1 tablespoon soft butter with 1 teaspoon grated orange rind, 2 to 3 teaspoons orange juice, ⅓ cup chopped walnuts. Spread over warm cake.

119

# Collectors' Desserts

While many of us pass up desserts nowadays, I feel sweets have their place, if for no other reason than the sense of luxury they give, the warm nostalgia they often produce. A bright little tart crowned with luscious red berries can lift my spirits on a gloomy day as easily as a fresh hairdo or a new hat.

This chapter seemed to grow and grow—and still many of our old-time favorites had to be eliminated. Instead, I've tried to include a cross section of the more unusual or special desserts friends have particularly enjoyed at our house. Among them are my most-beloved, the fruit or ice cream concoctions, as well as rich tortes and cakes, a number of fancy pies and tarts, a selection of unusual cookies.

# CAKES, COOKIES AND TORTES

## ALL-AMERICAN CHOCOLATE CAKE

*Worth the time and money you put into a homemade cake. The luscious dark frosting is fudge personified!*

- 2 cups sifted cake flour
- ⅛ teaspoon salt
- 3 squares unsweetened chocolate
- 4 eggs, separated
- 2 cups sugar
- ¾ cup butter
- 1 teaspoon vanilla
- 1 cup buttermilk
- 1 teaspoon soda
- 1 cup chopped walnuts
- 1 cup flaked coconut
  Real Fudge Frosting

Grease and flour lightly three 9-inch round layer cake pans. Sift flour with salt. Melt chocolate in small saucepan over very low heat. Separate eggs. Beat whites until stiff but not dry—the peaks will bend over slightly. Beat in 4 tablespoons of the sugar. Set aside. Cream butter until soft. Gradually beat in rest of sugar until very light and fluffy. Drop in egg yolks, one at a time, beating after each is added. Add vanilla. Beat until fluffy and light as whipped cream. Beat in chocolate. Now, stir in one-third of the flour. Mix buttermilk and soda; stir half of it into batter. Stir in another third of flour and then the rest of the milk. When smooth, add the last of the flour and beat until batter looks shiny and satiny. Gently fold in nuts, coconut and egg whites. Spread in pans. Bake at 350° about 30 minutes. Test with wire cake tester. Remove from oven, invert over wire racks, and let stand about 5 minutes. Loosen gently around edges with spatula, tilting pan to make sure cake is "free" as you lift off pans. Cool. Fill and frost with Real Fudge Frosting. Makes 16 servings.

May be baked in three 8-inch layers, if you prefer. It's also delicious filled with Vanilla Cream Filling (see index) and frosted as above.

121

*Real Fudge Frosting*
    2 whole eggs, beaten lightly
    2 cups sugar
    ½ cup cream or undiluted, evaporated milk
    4 squares unsweetened chocolate, melted
    2 tablespoons butter
    1½ teaspoons vanilla
    2 tablespoons boiling water

Mix together in medium saucepan: eggs, sugar, and cream. Bring to boil. Boil 3 minutes over low heat, stirring constantly. Remove from heat; add chocolate, butter and vanilla. Beat until creamy and cooled. When frosting becomes thick and hard to spread, beat in 1 tablespoon of the water until it becomes shiny again. Add rest of water in small portions as you work to keep frosting spreadable and glossy. Makes enough to fill and frost three 9-inch layers. (Cut recipe in half to use as frosting alone, or for smaller, two-layer cake.)

CHANTILLY TORTE

*Same batter as All-American Chocolate Cake—yet it's entirely different! Split into thin layers and spread with a whipped cream frosting, it becomes a very elegant, continental torte.*

Omit coconut and walnuts from batter for All-American Chocolate Cake. Bake in two, thicker 9-inch round layers at 350° about 35 to 40 minutes. Cool and carefully split with a serrated knife into 4 thin layers. Fill and frost with Whipped Cream Frosting. Top with curls of bitter or sweet chocolate.

*Whipped Cream Frosting*
    2 cups whipping cream
    4 tablespoons powdered sugar
      Pinch of mace
    1 teaspoon unflavored gelatin
    1½ teaspoons vanilla

In deep bowl, mix cream, sugar, and mace. Refrigerate an hour or more. Chill beater. Shortly before beating cream, put gelatin in small metal cup and sprinkle with 2 tablespoons cold water. Set in small pan of warm water to melt. Cool briefly, but it still must be melted. Whip cream mixture until very light and fluffy adding the melted gelatin as you beat. Flavor with vanilla.

NUT TORTE

*This rich continental dessert could make your party.*

> 1 cup ground walnuts
> 1 cup ground pecans
>      (about ¼ pound each of nutmeats)
> ½ teaspoon ground mace
> 1 cup fine zwiebach crumbs
> 6 egg whites (save three of the egg yolks for filling below)
> 3 egg yolks
> 1 cup sugar
>   Vanilla Cream Filling
>   Whipped cream and grated sweet chocolate for top

Line 2 8-inch layer cake pans with heavy brown paper. Grease well. Mix ground nuts, mace and crumbs. Beat egg whites stiff. With same beater, whip 3 egg yolks, then beat in sugar. Stir in nut-crumb mixture. Gradually fold this into egg whites. Spread in paper-lined pans. Bake at 325° 30 minutes. Turn out of pans onto wire racks to cool. Pull off paper at once. Cool and spread Vanilla Cream Filling between layers.

*Traditionally* the top is left plain, but you may like to add fluffs of whipped cream and a drift of grated chocolate. Cut in small wedges. Makes about 12 servings.

*Both torte and vanilla cream* may be made day before and put together day of party. Beat or stir filling before using.

> Vanilla Cream Filling
> > 1 cup cream
> > 1-inch piece vanilla bean or 1 teaspoon vanilla extract
> > 3 egg yolks from torte recipe
> ¼ cup sugar
> > 4 tablespoons flour
> >   Dash salt
> > 1 tablespoon brandy

Over very low heat scald cream with vanilla bean but do not boil (if extract is used, add later). In top of double boiler, stir egg yolks and sugar with wire whisk till well mixed. Blend in flour, salt and scalded cream. Cook and stir until it reaches the boiling point, *but do not boil.* Takes about 4 to 5 minutes and should be texture of heavy cream. Pour at once into small cold bowl to cool quickly. Add brandy (and extract if used). Stir occasionally till cold. Remove vanilla bean.

### CROWNED ANGEL

*Have you ever thought of baking an angel food cake with an upside-down topping? Do it in a ring mold.*

Blend 1 tablespoon honey into ¼ cup soft butter. Spread on bottom and sides of 9-inch salad ring mold. Sprinkle in ½ cup finely chopped, lightly toasted blanched almonds. Turn mold from side to side to coat with almonds. Prepare angel cake batter (you need only ½ regular home recipe or package of mix). Fill mold ⅔ full. (Bake left-over batter in a loaf or cupcakes.) Bake ring at 375° about 25 minutes. Invert over rack, remove at once to cool. Serve on a handsome cake stand. Heap center with sweetened whole berries.

### CLAIRE'S BOOZE CAKE

*Generous Claire Healey, a hard-working volunteer Gray Lady, must have served tons of this cake to appreciative servicemen in her tiny apartment overlooking San Francisco's Golden Gate! The boys called it Claire's Booze Cake and so it shall remain.*

1½ cups seedless raisins
2 cups water
½ cup shortening
¾ cup sugar
1 egg
1½ cups sifted all-purpose flour
1 teaspoon soda
½ teaspoon cloves
½ teaspoon nutmeg
¼ teaspoon allspice

½ teaspoon salt
1 cup chopped walnuts
2 tablespoons Bourbon whiskey

Cover raisins with water and simmer uncovered for 20 minutes. Drain, saving ¾ cup cooking liquid. Cool. Cream shortening and sugar together thoroughly. Beat in egg. Sift together flour, soda, spices and salt. Blend into creamed mixture alternately with cooking liquid. Stir in raisins, nuts, and whiskey. Pour into 2 greased 9-inch layer cake pans. Bake at 350° about 25 minutes. Remove from pans; cool thoroughly. Frost tops and sides with Bourbon Hard Sauce. Decorate top with walnut halves.

*Bourbon Hard Sauce*

¼ cup butter or margarine
3 cups sifted powdered sugar
1 egg
4 tablespoons Bourbon whiskey
Walnut halves

Cream butter and gradually beat in sugar alternately with lightly beaten egg and Bourbon.

*Sherry Raisin Cake (A Variation)*

Make exactly like Claire's Booze Cake except simmer the raisins in 2 cups sherry wine instead of water. Use ¾ cup of this liquid (cooled) in the cake and omit the 2 tablespoons Bourbon. Make frosting the same except again replace Bourbon with sherry.

## MOTHER'S PECAN APPLESAUCE CAKE

*Mother insists that this should be made with fresh applesauce. A holiday tradition since childhood—we hardly knew which we preferred, this of her fruitcake. This makes two cakes.*

1 cup raisins
1 cup fresh dates
1½ cups coarsely chopped pecans
4 cups sifted all-purpose flour

3 teaspoons soda
¾ teaspoon salt
1 teaspoon each cinnamon, nutmeg and allspice
1 cup shortening (part butter)
2 cups sugar
3 eggs
3 cups thick unsweetened applesauce
½ cup strawberry preserves
1 tablespoon brandy
1 teaspoon vanilla
   Hard-sauce frosting, if you like

Grease 2 metal loaf pans (9 x 5 x 3 inches). Rinse raisins; dry on paper towels. Cut dates from pits into small pieces. Prepare nuts. Sift together flour, soda, salt and spices. Cream shortening and sugar together till fluffy and smooth. Beat in eggs, one at a time. Add alternately, blending in each time, the flour and applesauce. Stir in preserves, fruits, nuts, brandy and vanilla. Turn into prepared pans. Bake at 350° 1 hour and 15 minutes, or until done when tested. Remove from pans and cool on wire rack. Frost with Hard Sauce and decorate with nuts and candied fruits.


FRUIT SOUR CREAM FILLING

*An uncooked cake filling, rich and easy and good with spice cake.*

1 cup dried figs
½ cup light or dark raisins
1 cup cooked prunes
¼ cup chopped maraschino cherries
1 cup sour cream
½ cup powdered sugar
1 cup chopped walnuts
1 tablespoon grated orange rind

Rinse figs and raisins in hot water. Cut figs into fine pieces. Cut prunes from pits into small pieces. Mix fruits, sour cream and sugar. Stir in walnuts and orange rind. Filling for a 3-layer cake.

BREEZEWAY SQUARES

*An unusual baked-on sour cream topping is a welcome change from gooey, fluffy frosting. Much easier to serve, too. Nice served warm, but if more convenient, bake ahead and serve at room temperature, or reheat.*

> Batter for your favorite chocolate cake
>     or 1 package chocolate cake mix
> 1½ cups sour cream
>     3 tablespoons sugar
>     1 teaspoon vanilla
>     ½ teaspoon cinnamon

Grease and dust with flour an oblong pan (13 x 9½ x 2 inches). Mix cake batter and pour into pan. Bake at 350° about 30 minutes. Remove cake from oven; let stand 10 minutes. Whip sour cream till fluffy. Beat in sugar, vanilla and cinnamon. Spread over cake in pan. Bake 10 minutes longer. Cut cake into squares and serve warm.

MAKE-BELIEVE CHEESE CAKE

*The idea for this concoction came from Helen Evans Brown, western food authority, and a wonderful friend. It's as creamy and rich as the real McCoy but so much easier to make. Serve with cold honey-sweetened berries, rosy rhubarb sauce or chunks of fresh pineapple.*

Cut poundcake into slices ½ inch thick. Spread one side and edges with sour cream, cover generously with brown sugar. Lay carefully, spread-side down in shallow pan or dish. Coat top sides with more sour cream and brown sugar. Sprinkle thickly with chopped toasted almonds. Leave in refrigerator 4 or 5 hours or overnight. Lift out onto serving plates with broad spatula. Allow one slice for each serving.

GEORGETOWN PUDDING

*Ideal for busy holidays since you can make and chill it days ahead!*

> 1 cup fine vanilla wafer crumbs
> 2 cups powdered sugar
> ¼ teaspoon salt

3 tablespoons cocoa
¼ pound soft butter
3 tablespoons brandy or dark rum
2 eggs, separated
1 teaspoon vanilla
1½ cups chopped walnuts
    Whipped cream

Line shallow oblong pan (large ice cube tray or pan about 6 x 8 inches) with strips of wax paper that extend over top of pan. Butter lightly and cover with half the crumbs. Sift together powdered sugar, salt, and cocoa. Cream butter and gradually beat in sugar until fluffy. Thin with up to 2 tablespoons brandy as you add sugar. Beat in egg yolks. Stir in vanilla and 1 cup chopped walnuts. Fold in stiffly beaten egg whites. Spread over crumbs. Top with rest of crumbs. Sprinkle with remainder of brandy, the last ½ cup walnuts. Chill overnight, or a couple of days. Serve in tiny, tiny squares with unsweetened whipped cream, and strong black coffee. Makes 8 to 12 servings.

AMANDINES

*Very distinctive in flavor—rich yet delicate!*

1 cup finely chopped blanched almonds
½ cup toasted sesame seeds
2½ cups sifted all-purpose flour
½ teaspoon salt
1 teaspoon baking powder
1 teaspoon ground cardamon
1 cup sugar
1 cup butter (or part margarine)
¼ cup honey
2 egg yolks
1 teaspoon vanilla

Prepare almonds. Spread sesame seeds in a shallow pan. Toast in moderate oven until golden, about 15 minutes. Sift together flour, salt, baking powder, and cardamon. Work sugar into soft butter until creamy. Stir in honey, egg yolks, vanilla, flour mixture, then almonds and sesame seeds. Refrigerate dough for easier handling. Shape into small balls, flatten and dip tops in sesame seeds, or chopped almonds. (Or shape in one of the variations suggested below). Bake at 350° 12 to 14 minutes, until light brown only. Makes about 5 dozen.

*For holidays, top each cooky with a candied cherry or almond before baking or shape into crescents and sprinkle with sesame seeds. Also delicious and showy baked in tiny balls and rolled in powdered sugar while warm.*

### APRICOT KOLACHKY

*Fragile cream cheese cookies. Ideal for holiday entertaining or a pretty tea. Extremely simple to make, too!*

> ½ cup butter
> 1 3-ounce package cream cheese
> 1 cup sifted all-purpose flour
> 1 cup apricot or cherry jam
> Powdered sugar

Cream butter and cheese together in mixer. Gradually work in flour. Roll out paper thin on floured board or pastry cloth. Cut with 2-inch round cutter. Spread with apricot or cherry jam. Fold two edges to center, overlapping slightly. Press down lightly with thumb. Place on greased cooky sheet. Bake at 375° 15 minutes. While warm sift powdered sugar over the top. Makes 3½ to 4 dozen.

### SUE'S AD LIB COOKIES

*Sue Johanson, who gave me this recipe, calls it "ad lib" because one can change ingredients according to whatever the cupboard provides. Among our teen-age friends, this is the most popular cooky I bake.*

> 2 cups sifted all-purpose flour
> ½ teaspoon baking powder
> ½ teaspoon soda
> Pinch salt
> 1 cup shortening
> 1 cup brown sugar, packed
> 1 cup granulated sugar
> 2 eggs
> 1 teaspoon vanilla

and any or all of the following:

> 1 cup uncooked oats
> 1 cup cornflakes—or ready-to-eat cereal
> 1 cup flaked coconut
> 1 cup chopped nuts
> 1 cup chocolate chips—or chopped dates

Sift together flour, baking powder, soda, and salt. Cream shortening and beat in sugars, until mixture is creamy. Beat in eggs, then stir in dry ingredients, vanilla, and rest of ingredients. Drop by teaspoonful onto greased cooky sheets. Bake at 350° 15 to 20 minutes. Cool on wire racks. Makes 5 to 6 dozen cookies.


VIENNESE PASTRY STRIPS

*Serve these colorful fruit glazed pastries for a special coffee party or brunch.*

> 2 3-ounce packages cream cheese
> ½ cup butter or margarine
> 2 cups sifted all-purpose flour
> ½ teaspoon salt
> 3 tablespoons cold milk or water
> 4 tablespoons sour cream
> 2 tablespoons brown sugar
> 4 tablespoons grated dry bread crumbs
> 3 to 4 fresh nectarines
> ¾ cup apricot preserves or orange marmalade

Work cream cheese and butter into flour and salt. Stir in milk. Ball up on waxed paper and chill overnight. Roll and fit into jelly roll pan (13 x 9). Spread with sour cream, sprinkle with brown sugar, then crumbs. Peel and slice nectarines. Arrange in even rows over crumbs. Spread with preserves. Bake in hot (425°) oven 20 to 25 minutes. Cut into strips 3 x 1½ inches. Serve warm or cold with coffee or tea. Makes about 2 dozen pastries.

## ENGLISH BUTTERSCOTCH STICKS

*These thin, rich cookies become crisp and lace-like when cool. They're extremely simple to make and contain no flour, but you may stir in 2 tablespoonsful if you prefer them a little less rich and fragile.*

Chop 1¼ cups uncooked rolled oats very finely, until they measure 1 cup. (Mouli grater or nut chopper is fine.) Blend ½ cup soft butter or margarine with ⅔ cup firmly packed light-brown sugar. Work in oats, ½ cup finely chopped, shredded coconut, ¼ cup chopped walnuts, a dash of salt and 1 teaspoon vanilla. Spread in jelly roll pan (13 x 9 inches). Bake at 350° about 20 minutes, until they have almost stopped bubbling. Cook for 10 minutes, then cut into sticks about 1 x 3 inches. Remove from pan when completely cold. Makes 3½ dozen.

## ANISE THINS

*Cream cheese and a few crushed anise seeds give a delicate and elusive flavor to these rich butter cookies, a Christmas tradition at our house.*

>     1 cup soft butter
>     1 3-ounce package cream cheese
>     1 cup sugar
>     1 egg yolk
>     ½ teaspoon vanilla
>     2½ cups sifted all-purpose flour
>     ½ teaspoon salt
>     2 teaspoons anise seeds, crushed

Mix together thoroughly butter, cream cheese, sugar, egg yolk, and vanilla. Combine flour, salt, and crushed anise seeds. Blend into butter mixture until smooth. On waxed paper form into two long rolls about 1½ inches in diameter. Wrap and chill about 2 hours. Slice ⅛ inch thick. With spatula lift onto ungreased cooky sheet. Bake in moderate oven (350°) 8 to 10 minutes, until golden and brown-rimmed. Do not brown, merely tan well. Overcooking spoils the delicate flavor and texture. Makes about 5 to 6 dozen thins.

*Cooky mix anise thins:* Blend 1 3-ounce package cream cheese into plain vanilla cooky mix). Stir in 1½ teaspoons crushed anise seeds, 1 tablespoon water or milk. Form into rolls on waxed paper. Chill, slice, and bake as above.

*For nutmeg wafers:* Replace anise seeds with 1 teaspoon nutmeg in either of the recipes above.

*For sesame crisps:* Replace anise seeds or nutmeg in above recipes with 2 tablespoons lightly toasted sesame seeds.

### ALMOND GOLD COOKIES

*Be careful not to overbake these, and remove immediately from cooky sheet. The sweet flavor of almonds comes through better after they have mellowed a bit.*

> 1½ cups blanched almonds
> 4 egg yolks
> 1 cup sugar
> 2 tablespoons flour
> 1 teaspoon vanilla
> ⅛ teaspoon almond extract
> Split blanched almonds

*Day before:* Blanch almonds. Drain on paper towels overnight. Next day, grind medium fine. Mix egg yolks with sugar, but do not beat. Stir in almonds, flour, flavorings. Divide into 3 pieces. Lay on waxed paper and form into rolls about 1½ inches thick. Chill well. (It's sticky.) Slice into thin cookies and put on cooky sheets. Top each with a split almond or dip tops in chopped almonds. Bake at 350° 10 to 12 minutes. Makes about 5 to 6 dozen tiny, dainty cookies. Excellent with eggnog or a glass of port.

### CHOCOLATE MERINGUE BARS

*These chewy cookies are topped with a brown sugar meringue before baking.*

> 1½ cups sifted all-purpose flour
> ½ teaspoon salt
> 1 teaspoon baking powder
> ½ cup shortening
> 1 cup granulated sugar

2 eggs
1 teaspoon vanilla
2 squares unsweetened chocolate, melted
1 egg white
1 cup brown sugar, sifted
1 cup chopped nuts or half coconut and half nuts

Sift together flour, salt, baking powder. Cream shortening and granulated sugar together. Beat in eggs and vanilla till fluffy. Stir in chocolate, then dry ingredients. Spread thin, no thicker than ½ inch, on a shallow jelly-roll-type pan. (Or use heavyduty foil to form a 12 x 16-inch pan with 1-inch sides. Place on cooky sheet before filling.) Beat egg white stiff then gradually beat in brown sugar. Spread over batter. Sprinkle with nuts; press lightly into meringue. Bake in moderately slow oven (325°) 30 minutes. Cool. Cut in thin bars, 1 x 3 inches. Makes 48 cookies.

## AMY WILSON'S SHORTBREAD
*Rice flour gives this rich traditional cooky a little different texture. It's said to be old and very authentic made this way.*

5 cups sifted all-purpose flour
1 cup fine, granulated sugar
½ cup rice flour (from health food store)
1 pound butter
1 teaspoon vanilla, if you like

Combine flour, sugar and rice flour. With finger tips work in butter and vanilla until it will form a mass or ball. Work on board until smooth. Roll ⅓ inch thick and cut into desired shapes. The traditional way is to spread in a shallow jelly-roll pan. Flatten smooth with a rolling pin and sprinkle top with granulated sugar. Bake in 350° oven about 30 minutes, until pale gold in color. Cut in squares or diamonds while hot. Let cool in pan. Makes dozens, depending on size and shape.

## MARVA'S EASY TOFFEE
*A heavenly confection. Expensive, but worth every penny! Marva makes it with pecans but I often use lightly-toasted almonds which are more traditional.*

133

1 large milk-chocolate bar (about 8 ounces)
1 cup finely chopped pecans or lightly toasted almonds
½ pound butter and margarine (1 cube each)
1 cup granulated sugar
Dash salt

Grind or grate chocolate with Mouli grater. Mix with finely chopped nuts. Butter generously a glass baking dish, 8 x 12 inches. Warm in oven a few minutes. Spread half the chocolate mixture evenly in dish so that it begins to melt. Put butter, sugar, and salt in skillet or heavy pan. Cook over low heat, stirring frequently until a deep, golden-amber color and a few drops form a hard, brittle ball in cold water (about 290° on your candy thermometer). It takes less than 10 minutes. Pour quickly over chocolate in dish, spreading it out smoothly. Top immediately with rest of chocolate and nuts. Smooth with a spatula dipped in hot water. Cool, then chill in refrigerator. Cut or break into tiny squares or pieces. Keep in refrigerator as chocolate is soft and creamy, and melts a little if too warm.

## PIES AND PASTRIES

### BASIC FLAKY PASTRY

*There isn't space in this book for all the details concerned with pastry making. However, this basic recipe for pastry seems in order. I find a canvas pastry cloth stretched on my board and a stockinet covering for the rolling pin a big help in rolling the dough. It completely eliminates stickiness, the need for extra flour and any overhandling. I use cold milk for the liquid in place of ice water. The milk is always chilled and seems to make the dough easier to handle. It also produces a richer brown crust.*

2 cups sifted all-purpose flour
1 teaspoon salt
⅔ cup shortening*
4 to 5 tablespoons cold milk

This makes enough for a two-crust pie or two single 9-inch crusts. Sift together flour and salt into bowl. Cut in half the shortening, until mixture is crumbly and texture of coarse meal. Cut in rest of shortening more coarsely, leaving pieces the size of small green peas.

Now sprinkle in liquid cautiously, a tablespoon at a time, but add enough or the dough will be impossible to handle and break into pieces when rolled. Mixing lightly and quickly with a fork, you have added enough when the dough forms a loose ball around the fork and leaves sides of bowl. Press waxed paper on top and cup dough gently in your palms to form a smooth ball.

It's easier to roll immediately—but on a warm day, chill it a half hour. Roll with quick light strokes, in one direction only. Re-rolled pastry will remain flaky and tender if you stack pieces, layer on layer, rather than wad them up in a ball.

*Use part butter or lard for the shortening if you like. For salad oil pastry, use a recipe written especially for that.

*Cream cheese pastry:* Cream together well, ½ cup sweet or regular butter and 1 3-ounce package cream cheese. With fork work in 1 cup sifted all-purpose flour and a dash of salt. When smooth, wrap in waxed paper and chill overnight. Ideal for tarts, small pastries.

CAPPY'S LEMON SOUFFLÉ PIE

*This is my favorite lemon pie. It's light and airy but not all fluff like a chiffon pie. It's been my sister Cappy's specialty for years.*

>  1 baked 9-inch pie shell
>  1 cup boiling water
>  1 tablespoon butter
>   Grated rind 1 lemon
>  5 eggs
> ¾ cup sugar
>  2 tablespoons cornstarch
>   Dash of salt
>  4 tablespoons lemon juice
>  6 tablespoons sugar for meringue
> ½ teaspoon vanilla

Bake and cool pie shell ahead of time. In top of double boiler over hot water, combine boiling water, butter and lemon rind. Separate eggs, putting two of the whites in a separate bowl. Beat yolks until thick. Mix sugar with cornstarch and salt. Slowly add to yolks. Beat till fluffy. Add lemon juice and mix slowly. Pour into boiling water mixture, stirring constantly. Cook and stir just until thick. *Do not overcook.* Cool while beating two of the egg whites until stiff. Fold into filling.

*Meringue:* Beat remaining 3 egg whites until frothy. Gradually beat in sugar, 1 tablespoon at a time. Continue beating until meringue stands in stiff peaks. Fold in vanilla. Pour filling into baked pie shell. Spread meringue over filling in deep, soft swirls so that it is anchored to the pastry all around to seal in the filling. Bake at 350° 12 to 15 minutes or until meringue is deep gold and tinged with brown.

### TINY TIM BUTTER TARTS

*Our young Canadian neighbor serves these easy little "pick-up pies" with tea. They're from an old English recipe.*

> 1 cup pastry recipe
> ⅓ cup butter (or part margarine)
> 1 cup sifted brown sugar
> 2 tablespoons milk or cream
> 1 beaten egg
> 1 teaspoon vanilla
> ¼ cup dark raisins, rinsed

Roll pastry thin and cut with scalloped 3-inch round cooky cutter. Or cut around a 3-inch glass or can with pastry wheel. Fit into 2-inch muffin pans so you'll have some dough on sides. Cream butter and sugar. Blend in rest of ingredients. Put 1 tablespoon filling in each tart. Bake at 450° about 7 minutes. Reduce heat to 350°. Bake 7 or 8 minutes longer. Makes 15 tiny tarts.

### GRAN'S RAISIN PIE

*Grinding the raisins gives this old-fashioned pie a deeper, fruitier taste. Simply add cream, sugar and lemon juice, and that's it.*

> 3 cups seedless raisins
> ½ cup sugar

1½ cups cream
¼ teaspoon salt
2 tablespoons lemon juice
Pastry for double 9-inch crust

Rinse raisins in hot water and drain thoroughly. Put through food chopper using medium blade. Combine with sugar, cream, and salt. Heat until sugar is dissolved. Blend in lemon juice. Pour into pastry-lined pie pan. Roll pastry for top, cut slits and place over filling. Pinch edges together to seal. Bake at 425° 10 minutes. Reduce heat to 375° and bake about 35 minutes longer. Serves 6 to 8.

### JAMAICA CHOCOLATE PIE

*It would be pretty difficult to make a better chocolate pie from scratch than this one made with a package of chocolate pudding mix! Extra chocolate, egg yolks, good dark rum and whipped cream are the secrets.*

Pastry for 8- or 9-inch crust
1 package chocolate pudding mix
1½ cups milk
2 egg yolks
¼ cup sugar
2 squares unsweetened chocolate, grated
3 tablespoons dark Jamaica rum
1 cup whipping cream
2 tablespoons powdered sugar
Shaved unsweetened or semi-sweet chocolate

Roll pastry and fit into 8- or 9-inch pie pan. Prick all over with fork. Bake at 475° 8 to 12 minutes. Cool. Combine pudding mix and milk in saucepan. Stir over medium heat until it boils and thickens. Remove from heat. Stir in slightly beaten egg yolks, sugar, grated chocolate and 2 tablespoons rum. Cover to avoid film on top. Cool. Whip cream and fold half of it into cooled filling. Spread in baked pie shell. Fold powdered sugar and rum into rest of whipped cream. Swirl over top of filling. Sprinkle top with shaved chocolate (made with potato peeler). Chill completely before cutting.

PEACH PIE IN ALMOND SHELL

*Extravagant and rich, but easy to make.*

Coconut Almond Shell:

    1 cup blanched almonds
    1 cup moist-style flaked coconut
    ¼ cup sugar
    ¼ cup butter or margarine

Filling:

    1 cup sour cream
    6 tablespoons powdered sugar
    1 teaspoon orange juice
    1 teaspoon shredded orange rind
    1 teaspoon vanilla
    3 cups drained sliced peaches, canned or fresh
    ½ cup whipping cream

Grind almonds medium fine. Mix with coconut. Work in sugar and butter with fingers or spoon. Press evenly in bottom and sides of 9-inch glass pie plate, saving 2 or 3 tablespoons crumbly mixture for top. Bake at 375° until light golden brown, 12 to 15 minutes. Put topping crumbs in shallow pan. Toast in oven at same time, about 5 minutes. Cool.

*One hour before serving* beat sour cream lightly with fork. Add dash of salt, 4 tablespoons powdered sugar, orange juice, rind and vanilla. Spread on bottom and sides of shell. Cover with peaches. Whip cream until thick and fluffy; fold in remaining 2 tablespoons sugar. Swirl lightly over peaches. Sprinkle with toasted topping. Chill. Cut in small wedges.


MY PUMPKIN PIE

*This looks like any other pumpkin pie, but the addition of corn syrup and a smaller amount of sugar gives a smoother textured pie—a lighter, more subtle flavor. I worked it out during World War II when sugar was short—and have given it to scores of friends since. Partially baking the pastry insures a crisp bottom crust.*

1 unbaked 9-inch pie shell
1½ cups undiluted evaporated milk
⅔ cup firmly packed brown sugar
¼ cup light corn syrup
½ teaspoon salt
½ teaspoon allspice
½ teaspoon cinnamon
½ teaspoon nutmeg
¼ teaspoon ginger
1½ cups canned pumpkin
2 eggs, lightly beaten

Make pie shell ahead of time. Scald milk. Stir brown sugar, corn syrup, salt, spices into pumpkin. Stir in lightly beaten eggs and milk. Brush pastry shell with egg white. Bake at 450° until it starts to brown, 6 to 8 minutes. Without removing from oven, slide rack out part way and carefully pour pumpkin filling into partially baked pastry. (This more than fills the shell—we always look forward to little pumpkin custards.) Reduce heat to 300°. Bake 45 to 50 minutes, until center is not quite firm. (It continues to cook after it's out of the oven.) Cool.

STRAWBERRY CHEESE FLAN

*A beautiful French fruit tart that's easy to make.*

*Flan Shell:*

1 cup sifted all-purpose flour
¼ teaspoon salt
6 tablespoons sweet butter
1½ tablespoons sugar
1 egg yolk
1 tablespoon cold water or lemon juice
4 tablespoons grated almonds
2 3-ounce packages cream cheese
⅓ cup powdered sugar
⅓ cup sour cream
2 teaspoons grated orange rind
2 to 3 cups whole fresh strawberries

139

½ cup guava or red currant jelly
1 tablespoon Cointreau or orange Curaçao

*Flan Shell:* Sift together flour and salt. Beat butter, sugar and egg yolk until light. Work in flour, liquid and almonds. Chill in waxed paper 1 hour. Roll ⅛ inch thick. Fit into flan ring* (or 9-inch pie pan). Bake at 400° until light golden brown, about 15 minutes. Cool.

Soften cream cheese; mix in sugar, sour cream and orange rind. Spread in cooled flan shell. Top with strawberries. Melt jelly over low heat with the liqueur. Cool slightly. Spoon over berries to glaze. Chill until set. If you like, decorate around edges with whipped cream and toasted almonds.

*\*To improvise a flan ring:* Fold heavy-duty foil into about 6 layers of 1-inch width. Shape into a 9-inch ring. Fasten with a paper clip. Place on cooky sheet.

FRENCH DATE PIE

*This is delicious and very simple and fast to put together.*

Pastry for one 9-inch crust
1 cup fresh dates
3 eggs
½ teaspoon cornstarch
Dash of salt
½ teaspoon freshly grated nutmeg
¾ cup brown sugar (packed)
1 cup cream
1 teaspoon vanilla

Line pie plate with pastry; flute or crimp edges. Pit and slice dates into pastry-lined pan. Beat eggs enough to mix well. Blend cornstarch, salt and nutmeg into brown sugar. Stir into eggs, then blend in cream and vanilla. Pour into pastry shell. Bake at 450° 10 minutes. Reduce heat to 350°. Bake 20 to 25 minutes longer, until firm around edges when tested with a knife—but still a little quivery in the center. Cool completely before cutting.

## RASPBERRY MACAROON PIE

*An exotic pie. Easier to make than the telling!*

    1 baked 9-inch pie shell
    1½ cups sweetened raspberries, fresh or frozen
    1 envelope unflavored gelatin
    ⅓ cup sugar
    1¼ cups orange juice
    1 pint vanilla ice cream
    2 teaspoons Cointreau
    1 teaspoon grated orange rind
    1 cup dry macaroon crumbs
    Whipped cream

Bake and cool pie shell. Rinse and sweeten to taste fresh raspberries or barely defrost frozen ones. In 1½-quart saucepan mix gelatin, sugar and orange juice. Heat very slowly until gelatin and sugar are melted. Remove from heat, add ice cream by spoonsful. Stir until melted. Add Cointreau and orange rind. Chill until thick but not set. Fold in 1 cup raspberries and the macaroon crumbs. Chill till mixture will mound softly. Spoon into pie shell. Chill till set. Decorate top with rest of the berries and little puffs of whipped cream, if you like. Cut into small wedges.

## SAUCY PEACH PIE

*A spicy warm dessert like grandmothers' fragrant peach cobblers of long ago. Slip it in the oven a half hour before the dinner is ready. Then carry to the table after dinner, hot and juicy.*

    8 to 10 large canned cling peach halves
    ¾ cup peach syrup
    1 teaspoon shredded lemon rind
    ½ teaspoon cloves
    ¼ teaspoon nutmeg
    2 tablespoons butter or margarine
    ⅓ cup sugar
    2 teaspoons cornstarch
    ⅓ cup sherry wine (or orange juice)
    1½ cup recipe rich shortcake or biscuit dough

141

Drain peaches and combine ¾ cup of the peach syrup with lemon rind, spices, butter, and sugar and cornstarch blended together. Simmer 5 minutes. Add wine or orange juice. Roll rich dough on floured pastry cloth or board into 12-inch square. Fit into round glass baking dish (8½ inches wide, 2 inches deep). Let corners hang over edge. Fill with peaches, cut side up. Pour two-thirds of boiling hot sauce over fruit, then fold corners of dough towards center. Pour rest of sauce on top. Bake at 425° 15 minutes. Reduce heat to moderate. Bake 20 minutes longer, or until golden brown and glazed. Serve warm. It's gilding the lily, but this is luscious with a trickle of cream poured over it. Serves 6.

*Fresh Peach Pie:* Use 10 large halves, ¾ cup water, ⅔ cup sugar.

# FRUITS, CUSTARDS AND ICES

## BOUQUET COMPOTE

*Fresh fruits in an orange syrup delicately laced with Curacao. What could be cooler or more elegant after a rich dinner?*

>    4 large oranges
>    1 cup sugar
>    1 cup water
>    ¼ cup Orange Curaçao or Triple Sec, if desired
>    1 tablespoon lemon juice
>    1 cup seedless green grapes
> 1½ cups watermelon balls or whole strawberries
>     Bunch of fresh mint or lime or lemon sherbet

Peel oranges round and round with a sharp knife, cutting away all white membrane. Cut enough yellow peel into tiny match-sticks to measure 4 tablespoons. Cover with cold water; simmer 5 minutes. Drain and rinse. Combine with the 1 cup sugar and water. Simmer gently without stirring for 12 minutes. Quarter oranges, slice crosswise. Add Curaçao, hot syrup and orange slivers. Cool slightly and add lemon juice, grapes and melon balls. Chill several hours. Serve with a topknot of fresh mint or with balls of lemon or lime sherbet. Makes 4 or 5 servings.

## FRUITS ANISETTA

*A few crushed anise seeds in the port wine sauce give a new flavor to this hot fruit compote. Serve it with the contrast of a dollop of very cold sour cream.*

> 6 to 8 large peach halves, canned or fresh
> 1 can Bing cherries (2 cups)
> 1½ tablespoons butter
> 1 cup port wine
> 3 tablespoons sugar
> 1 teaspoon grated lemon rind
> 1 2-inch stick cinnamon
> ¼ teaspoon anise seeds
> ⅓ cup toasted almond slivers

Drain peaches and cherries, saving 1 cup syrup from cherries. (Peel and halve fresh peaches.) Lay peaches in shallow baking dish; put dot of butter and a cherry in each. Pour rest of cherries around peaches. Mix wine, sugar (use ⅓ cup for fresh peaches), lemon rind, fruit syrup, cinnamon and anise seeds. Boil 2 or 3 minutes. Pour over fruit. Bake at 350° 25 minutes, or until bubbly hot. Baste peaches with sauce frequently. Let cool till just warm, spooning sauce over fruit from time to time. Sprinkle with almonds. Serve with very cold whipped or sour cream. Serves six.

## CELESTIAL FRUITS

*Fruits, brown sugar and sour cream mellowed in the refrigerator. Utter simplicity—great elegance!*

> 2 cups peaches or nectarines
> 2 cups seedless green grapes
> 1½ cups thick sour cream
> ½ cup brown sugar
> Grated fresh coconut (or moist-style flaked)

Cut peaches or nectarines into bite-size pieces. Wash grapes and pull from stems. In a pretty glass serving bowl, place a layer of half the fruits.

143

Top with half the sour cream and brown sugar. Cover with the rest of the brown sugar and spread the sour cream in a smooth layer over the top. Chill in the refrigerator 4 to 6 hours, until icy cold and the brown sugar-sour cream sauce has mellowed down into the fruits. Decorate with a shower of snowy white coconut. Serves 4 to 6. Good with lady fingers or thin, crisp cookies.


STUFFED MELON

*Summer in a melon! A beautiful luncheon salad or a jumbo dessert.*

>    2 medium cantaloupes
>    2 cups fresh pineapple, in bite-size pieces
>    1 cup seedless green grapes
>       Grated rind and juice of 1 orange
>    ¼ cup honey
>    2 teaspoons fresh lemon juice
>    1 cup flaked coconut
>    ¼ cup dark Jamaica rum
>    1 cup fresh berries (strawberries, raspberries, blueberries)
>       Sour cream or sherbet

Halve cantaloupes; remove seeds. With melon-ball cutter or ½ teaspoon measure, cut out one row of balls around edge of cavity. Mix with pineapple, grapes. Grate orange rind over frruits. Add orange juice to honey, lemon juice, coconut and rum. Mix with fruits (not berries yet). Chill. Set cantaloupe halves on frosty mint-decorated plates. Add berries to fruits; heap into cantaloupe. For salad, top with sour cream. For a jumbo dessert, add a peak of sherbet. Makes 4. Serve with a spoon so you can dig out all the sweet cantaloupe.


BAKED PEARS SAYBAYON

*The contrast of blazing hot pears and a very cold wine custard is delightful.*

>    3 egg yolks
>    1½ tablespoons sugar

⅓ cup sherry wine
8 large pear halves, canned or fresh
2 tablespoons butter, melted
2 tablespoons sugar
8 macaroons
¼ cup blanched almond halves
  Grated nutmeg

*Make sherry sauce ahead:* In top of double boiler, away from heat, beat egg yolks and sugar with wire whisk or rotary beater till light and fluffy. Gradually beat in sherry. Put just enough hot water in bottom of double boiler so that top pan does not touch it. Put boiler together and place over low heat. Stir sauce with a wire whisk over *hot*, not boiling, water until smooth and thick, 5 to 7 minutes. Refrigerate, covered, until ice cold. If it separates, simply stir again till smooth. Place pears in shallow baking dish with 2 or 3 tablespoons fruit syrup or water. Coat with melted butter, sprinkle with sugar (use ¼ cup sugar for fresh pears). Crumble macaroons into centers. Toss almonds in a little melted butter and sprinkle on top. Bake at 350° 20 to 30 minutes. Baste occasionally. Serve hot with ice cold sherry sauce. Grate fresh nutmeg over top. Makes 4 to 6 servings.

## JENNIE KIMBALL'S CUSTARD

*A delicate, not-sweet custard that never separates, if you follow the directions. The proportions are easy to remember, no matter how large a recipe you make—1 egg, 1 tablespoon sugar, 1 cup milk.*

4 eggs
4 tablespoons sugar
4 cups milk
2 teaspoons vanilla
½ teaspoon almond extract
  Freshly grated nutmeg

Beat eggs enough to mix yolks and whites well. Beat in sugar (round the spoon if you like it sweeter but we think it's perfect this way). Stir in milk and seasonings. Pour into 1½-quart baking dish. Set in pan con-

145

taining ½ inch water. Cook at 350° at least 30 minutes or until a silver knife stuck into the side (not center) is clean looking when removed. Cool. Chill and spoon into serving dishes. Serve plain or with a topping of berries or other fruits. Makes 6 servings.

*Raisin rice custard:* Add to mixed custard before baking, ½ cup cooked rice and a handful of raisins.


## EXOTIC ICE CREAM

Using a fork, quickly stir into a quart of vanilla ice cream: 4 tablespoons Crème de Cacao, ¼ cup chopped candied cherries or *marrons glacés* (candied chestnuts), ½ cup flaked coconut. Refreeze till firm or nearly so. Serve in tea cups or small glasses with shaved chocolate on top.


## PRALINED PLUMS

     1 can purple plums (1 lb. 13 oz.)
     ¼ cup sugar
     ½ teaspoon cinnamon
     1 2-inch spiral lemon peel
     2 tablespoons favorite liqueur or sherry wine
     ⅓ cup chopped almonds
     1 tablespoon butter or margarine
     2 tablespoons dark brown sugar
     Vanilla ice cream

Gently heat plums with sugar, cinnamon, and lemon peel in moderate oven or over low heat. Sprinkle with the liqueur or sherry. In heavy skillet mix almonds, butter and brown sugar. Stir over medium heat 3 to 5 minutes, until mixture smells "buttery" and looks bubbly-brown. Turn onto a cold plate and cool a few minutes. Top each serving of warm plums with a scoop of ice cream. Crumble almond crunch lightly with finger tips and sprinkle on top. Makes 4 servings.


## CONTINENTAL COMPOTE, SAUCE ROMANOFF

*An impressively beautiful and elegant dessert. Fruits poached in a vanilla syrup and served with a heavenly ice cream sauce.*

Combine 2 cups water, 1 cup sugar, a 1-inch piece of vanilla bean, split and scraped. Simmer 5 minutes. Add 8 to 10 peeled, fresh fruit (peach halves, whole nectarines, pears, or apricots—all are nice—or a combination of several). Poach gently, basting occasionally, until fruit is cooked but still shapely—8 to 10 minutes. Remove fruits to crystal bowl; add 1 tablespoon each of brandy and Grand Marnier or kirsch. Simmer syrup another minute or two to thicken slightly. Pour over fruits. An hour before serving, add a dozen whole strawberries or a cup of fresh blueberries. Serve with Sauce Romanoff. Makes 6 servings.

*Sauce Romanoff:* Soften a quart of good vanilla ice cream and quickly beat in 3 tablespoons brandy. Fold in 1 cup heavy cream, whipped until thick. Return to freezer to become firm again. Serve in separate bowl.

RUM ICE IN LEMON SHELLS

*For a really dramatic effect, bank this dessert in a bed of chipped ice studded with white gardenias and shiny green leaves.*
    *My thanks to Sunkist who gave me the basic lemon sherbet recipe which I've revised as below:*

        1 cup sugar
        2 teaspoons unflavored gelatin
    1¾ cups milk
    ¼ cup white rum
        2 teaspoons finely grated lemon peel
    ⅔ cup fresh lemon juice
        Dash salt
    6 to 8 large lemons or oranges for shells
        2 unbeaten egg whites

Turn refrigerator control to coldest position. Mix sugar, gelatin and milk. Stir over very low heat till gelatin is melted and milk scalding hot. Do not boil. Add rum, and set aside to cool, otherwise it will curdle when you add lemon. Slowly stir in lemon peel, juice and salt. Pour into 2 small or 1 large freezing tray and freeze till mushy. Meanwhile, cut tops off large perfect lemons or oranges. Both are good and each gives a little different perfume to the sherbet. With a grapefruit knife and spoon, remove pulp. Cut a thin slice from bottom of lemon so it will stand upright. Put mushy sherbet in chilled bowl with unbeaten egg whites. Beat until light and fluffy. Heap into lemon or orange shells. Freeze overnight, with control at normal. Remove from freezer 15 minutes before serving.

## CAFÉ JAMAICA

On a trip to Mexico City, we met Enrique, half French, half Mexican air lines pilot who took us to a Swiss restaurant for dinner. There he ordered Café Jamaica for dessert. It sounded exciting to us, and looked even more so when it arrived in coffee cups.

I didn't get the recipe, but this is how it tasted to me. A heady concoction of coffee, dark rum and cream which you half eat, half drink.

> 1 quart best-quality coffee ice cream
> 1 teaspoon instant powdered coffee
> 6 tablespoons dark Jamaica rum
> ½ cup whipping cream

Buy the very best, *hard* coffee ice cream you can find. (The airy, cheaper kinds won't stand up for this treatment.) For deeper coffee flavor, dissolve the instant coffee in a little of the rum. Then, working quickly, blend rum into ice cream with fork. It will soften as you work but try to keep it from getting too liquefied. Return to freezer and freeze again. It won't freeze completely firm; it's supposed to be served a little soft. Just before serving, whip cream until thick and nearly stiff. Ripple quickly into ice cream. Spoon into small tea or coffee cups. Serve with a spoon. Makes 6 servings. A *grande finale*.

# Index